DENIM AND LACE
(AND A WHOLE LOT OF GRACE)

THIS BOOK IS DEDICATED TO:

our husbands,
Robert and Jim,
who loved us through it all

our friends, who stood by us while we "grew"

our pastors, who put up with us

AND MOST OF ALL:

Denim and Lace *is dedicated to our Lord, whose love,*
faithfulness and extended grace made it all possible.

The Struggles of a Friendship . . .

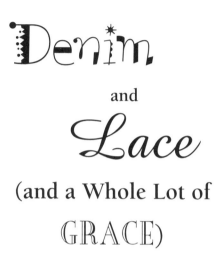

Denim

and

Lace

(and a Whole Lot of

GRACE)

Lois Olmstead
and Phyllis Rowe

HORIZON BOOKS
A division of Christian Publications, Inc.
CAMP HILL, PENNSYLVANIA

HORIZON BOOKS

a division of Christian Publications, Inc.

3825 Hartzdale Drive
Camp Hill, PA 17011
www.cpi-horizon.com
www.christianpublications.com

Denim and Lace and a Whole Lot of Grace
ISBN: 0-88965-197-3

LOC Control Number: 2001-131294

Contents

Denim and Lace

You created us, Lord
You called us by name
Each one is different
No two are the same
Molded in Your image
Walking in Your grace
We're Sunflowers or Roses
We are Denim—and we are Lace.

Phyllis Rowe © 2000

Introduction

One day the door opened and Lois walked into the ceramic shop where Phyllis was working. Then God started *His* work in the hearts and lives of these two ladies, one who knew Jesus and one who didn't.

One was a morning person,
   one a night person.
      One liked denim,
         one liked lace.
            One loved buttermilk,
               the other wouldn't get near the stuff.

Can God mold and form a friendship between these two women that He can use?

* * *

1

Phyllis Rowe was born into a family of five girls. From the hills and hollers of West Virginia, she moved to Butte, Montana and then to the eastern plains surrounding Colstrip. She tells of the rough roads of life and the potholes in those roads. Married at sixteen, Phyllis shares the heartache of an abusive marriage, raising two sons and dealing with the anger and bitterness that were some of the potholes.

Only a person who has traveled this road can know the blessing of peace that comes from overcoming such troubles. Phyllis is a gifted soloist, sharing many feelings and stories through her music. She loves licorice and buttermilk (together!) and adores being a grandmother. Her hobbies include writing poetry and collecting old barn pictures.

Lois Olmstead has traveled all over the country sharing her faith in God and her optimistic and often amusing views on life. Born and raised on a ranch near Livingston, Montana, Lois has always lived a full and interesting life. She's owned a gift shop, hosted and produced a daily half-hour radio program, worked as a receptionist, a bookkeeper, a tour guide and a County Extension Agent.

From her home in Colstrip, Montana, Lois currently writes a weekly column for the *Rosebud County Press.* She is the author of several books. Lois' witty and sensitive outlook is a gift she shares with many in need of a new way of looking at and coping with their lives. Her hobbies are sewing, raising ducks, painting and Native American beadwork. She loves being a grandmother.

* * *

Introduction

This glimpse into the lives of these two women was birthed into a seminar which they have shared in many communities and cities. The Denim and Lace Seminar is a wonderful place where women come expecting to laugh (and maybe cry) as these two share what friendships of women are really like. (And it isn't always sweet as apple pie!) Women leave the seminar with a better understanding of how to fix broken relationships, how to see themselves as others see them and how to live a life with uplifting friendships with others. God has used these two women as catalysts in healing the hurts in hundreds of lives. This book will take you to that seminar. Pray that God will use their experience to touch your life as well.

1

Women Are Unique

Lois: Women are so unique. I have never in my life gone into a restaurant and heard one man say to another, "Do you have to go to the bathroom?" I have never heard a man get ready to go somewhere and ask another man, "What are you going to wear?"

When Phyllis and I leave for a seminar, we always have to check on our clothing plans. Otherwise it will happen like it did today: I went to pick Phyllis up. She looked at me and said, "Oh, you've got jeans on." Then she disappeared into her bathroom and soon came back with jeans on. Then we could proceed with our trip. And you should see us packing!

Phyllis: I packed to go to a retreat in Williston, North Dakota for two days. I looked at the pile of stuff that I would need. There was the music stuff: the sound system for my backup tapes, the song sheets and notebooks with words of songs and the microphones and cords. There was my notebook and Bible. There was the bag of treats and goodies (an absolute must!). My purse. My clothes bag. It all seemed to be there, but as I looked at my clothes bag I did think I should try to lighten the load a little. I took inventory to see what could be eliminated. There were two sweaters (short sleeves), two pullovers, two turtlenecks and one sweater (long sleeves). There was the sweatshirt I was wearing. I had packed three pairs of pants. Jeans (with elastic waist), dress pants (in case I wanted to dress up) and the wrinkle-free pants. And the jeans I had on. There were four pairs of shoes. And the shoes I had on. I had pajamas (one short pair and one long pair) and one blazer and one nylon jacket. For two days.

Surely I didn't need all that! I decided I could eliminate the green turtleneck. I took it out of the bag and put it away in the bedroom. Then, with a quick change of heart, I promptly pulled off the sweatshirt I had on, put the green turtleneck on and put the sweatshirt back on. I was ready to go. My ride was waiting.

Why did I pack so much stuff! I asked myself as I rode along.

Well, first of all I didn't know what to expect as far as the weather goes. Hot? Cold? The motel itself—too stuffy or too drafty? What about my mood? Maybe I would feel like dressing up, maybe I would just want to wrap up in something warm and comfortable. What if I spilled something on myself? And then . . . I just like clothes. It doesn't matter if they come from yard sales or the best department stores—I just like clothes. But I had definitely packed a lot of stuff.

And then I realized there is a lot of other *stuff* we can pack that we don't really need. What about guilt or shame? What about grief, sorrow or sadness? What about anger, hurt, resentment or bitterness? What about fear, worry or stress? What about pride, self-righteousness or criticism? Jealousy? Envy? Unforgiveness? Do we lug any of these around with us?

What does Jesus say about the loads we are packing? In Bible study a couple weeks ago, we discussed Matthew 11:28-30, which says, "Come to Me, all you who labor and are heavy laden, and I will give you rest. Take My yoke upon you and learn from Me, for I am gentle and lowly in heart, and you will find rest for your souls. For My yoke is easy and My burden is light" (NKJV).

I realized my full clothes bag was not the only load I was packing. I told God there were a couple of things I wanted to leave in Williston. I was packing something I did not need.

How about you? As you begin this book, are you packing too much? Right now, you may need to stop and spend some time with the Lord. Tell Him you want to leave your burdens with Him. You can even ask Him to use this book and our experiences to help you lighten your load!

ois: Another good thing about women is that we are never afraid to tell about the dumb things we do. We just can't wait to call up another friend and tell her all about it. I have never heard Robert call Jim or another friend and say, "Oh, you will *never* believe what dumb thing I did this morning! Ha ha ha!" It just doesn't happen.

That is why we, the wives of those dear men, have to tell the stories on them.

Like just finding a simple place to park in a mall parking lot!

The husband and wife arrive in the family vehicle at the mall parking lot. The parking lot has spaces for 1,200 cars, give or take a few. This morning there are several empty spaces. He-who-is-driving turns into the wide middle aisle. There are two empty spots on this end. She-who-must-not-tell-him-how-to-drive says nothing as he drives by the empty spots. She just sets her lips in a straight line.

Another spot is open halfway down the lane. She-who slants her shoulder slightly to the left to prepare for his turn into the spot and then stiffly straightens up as He-who drives on. There is one on the right two car-lengths down. Just as He-who puts on the brakes to pull into the spot, a little red coupe cuts the corner and dives into the spot.

"Those little cars ought to be outlawed," says He-who.

"I think there is one right over there," says She-who, breaking her oath to not say one word about driving or parking on this day.

"I don't like to park over there. Those trees drip sap on the pickup."

There must be a secret homing device for each man for his particular vehicle, thinks the woman to herself. *The male bird cannot rest until he is at his own nest which has a secret beeper heard only by the male of the species.* "Hmmmmm."

"Hmmmmm what? I couldn't park there! Didn't you see that dented and beat-up truck parked right there? No telling how they would back out of that spot!"

"Hon, I didn't hmmmm you. I was just hmmmm-ing to myself."

"Oh well, here's one. Finally. Now, what did you have to do here?"

"I just have to drop these glasses off. It will only take a minute."

* * *

God made men and women different. He must have, because men just think differently than women. They do things differently too. First, let me say that I am not men-bashing. It's just that I really do believe women are unique.

Vacation time is approaching. I thought I should write about some of the hazards of traveling with your spouse. And I love my spouse.

But . . . when we travel, we have a few "difficulties." Our trip to Florida in December was no exception. We had a beautiful flight. But the minute we landed in Tampa, I knew it would happen again, just like it did in Los Angeles, Dallas, San Diego and Baton Rouge.

We present our papers for a rental car—that he reserved—and load our bags into the car. He gets behind the wheel of whatever snappy new model he has dreamed about driving for weeks and puts it in gear. We immediately head out of the commotion-filled car lot into the bumper-to-bumper four-lane traffic of a busy airport. He sees a car-length of open space in the race of hundreds of cars driving over the speed limit and zips us up into the line of traffic.

I hang on to the console and my door handle while overhead exit signs list fourteen options. I diligently try to read each one as designated trip-navigator with the highlighted Avis map on my lap.

But the driver. Is he reading the signs? *No.* He is trying the automatic rearview mirror buttons on the door armrest. From there he moves to the air-conditioner. We are zapped with high cool, low fan, medium temperature, maximum breeze and open vent as he pushes buttons. He moves from there to the steering wheel. The wheel tilts from the dash to his lap as six positions are tested. All the while we are the merg-er and merg-ee in the race for the airport exit. If I yell "Now!" at the appropriate time, we maneuver onto the packed freeway.

"Today in Tampa we have overcast skies and later we can expect . . . be-bop-a-do, oh, how I love . . . then if you have termites you can call . . . friends in low places . . . in Washington D.C. the President said . . . my achy breaky heart . . . " He is trying out the radio! The station digits race as fast as the 6 million cars behind us.

Just as I think he has tried every button, the seat moves. Up, down, back. The headrest tilts. The windows whoosh down as the automatic door lock by my shoulder clicks shut. Just as I am trying to find a street sign that matches one on the sweaty map in my lap, the dome light comes on and the visor comes down.

"Look at this, hon," he says, "a lighted mirror! Great, huh?"

Now, you see, if I were driving this car, we'd still be at the airport in the rental lot. I'd have to be checking out our route, adjusting the mirrors and fastening my seat belt. With him, we are already on our way . . . where we are I am not exactly sure. I cannot read the map when I am terrified out of my mind.

So now we could be lost. No, I mean *I* could be lost. Men never get lost. But that's another story.

I love you, Robert!

* * *

That is definitely not to say that I don't do dumb things. I wrote about that in *Breast Cancer and Me:*

Even before chemotherapy was in my life, I sometimes lacked concentration. One day I went to the laundry room and prepared to do my washing. I started the water in the machine and then went into the bedroom to get our dirty clothes out of the hamper. Two hours later I walked by the washer. Sure enough, it had gone through the whole cycle with no clothes in it. Somewhere between the washer and the bedroom I got sidetracked. I told my husband I had run the washer on a "cleaning cycle."

Another time a friend came by my house to pick me up to go out for coffee. She went out the door first and headed down the sidewalk. I thought she was taking the long way around to get over a large snowdrift in front of our house. I had my knee-high snowboots on so I just plowed through the drift. I got in the car and sat down.

Hmmm. I never noticed their upholstery is the same as in our car, I thought as I waited for my friend. *They even have a tape case like ours.* Then my brain engaged. I was sitting in our car on the passenger side, seat belt fastened. My friend was sitting in her car behind ours, wondering what in the world I was doing. (In my defense, both cars were blue!)

And that isn't all. We joined another friend for coffee. After visiting awhile, she said, "Lois, why are you wearing only one earring?" Grabbing my ear, I discovered she was right. I had no earring on one ear . . . but the other ear had an earring with two backs on it! I made a mental note right then to watch myself more carefully!

I am always getting up to go get something in the house and when I get there, I can't remember what I came for. (pages 206-207)

So far be it for me to deny doing dumb things—and there is something in me (being a woman?) that makes me just love to tell all this stuff to someone else!

❄ ❄ ❄

Women are different. Just like a flower garden, there is beauty in the differences. God made each one of us unique. He tells us so in His Word, the Bible. We believe the Bible is the inspired Word of God. It tells the stories of the lives of real women and real men. People just like us. Naomi was a real person. Elizabeth was a real person. So were Ruth and Esther and Dorcas and Eve. These were real, living women. And Joseph, David, Jehoshaphat and Peter were real people too. The Bible tells us their stories. We would like to tell you our story.

2

Up a Crick and Down a Holler

Lois: I learned about God when I was young. I was born on a ranch north of Livingston, Montana. I have one brother.

As a family, we worked together and we played together. We were a close family with lots of relatives nearby. On some weekends, we'd load the horses into a trailer and head for a rodeo. My dad rode bulls. Later my brother became a champion calf roper. I did some barrel racing. I was not a champion.

When I was about ten years old, my mom and dad went to hear a speaker at a church in town. They came home to tell us that they had surrendered their lives to the Lord, that they had been "saved." I didn't know exactly what that meant, but our lives changed.

I saw my mom become concerned about friends and relatives, telling them about Jesus. Jesus was her Friend. God gave her a compassion for others and a willingness to help anyone, anytime. She was always ready to help out at our church, the Livingston Bible Church, whenever there was a need, even though she was busy at home as well. I can remember her often praying, "Lord, just help us get the work done!"

My dad changed too. He had often had trouble with a temper. I saw that change as he fell humbly before the Lord. There was failure after failure at first. Then victory. Back then, I don't remember a night growing up that I didn't see him on his knees by the footstool in the living room praying before he went to bed.

In the morning when I would get up, and even with lots of chores to do, there would be my mom and dad, reading the Bible and having devotions. Our weekends changed too. Now we would go to church first, and then we would load the horse trailer and head out for the rodeos.

We went to church a lot. I memorized many Bible verses and Sunday school songs; I was always trying to be good! Many times I made trips to the altar pledging to be better. Those trips to the altar usually had something to do with sin and my brother.

You see, we had a ditch that ran between the house and the barn. I would go out and jump across that ditch. Being tall and thin and two years older, I could easily jump to the bank on the other side. Then I'd say, "Come on, Ronnie, you can do it!" With lots of encouragement, he'd try . . . and fall in. He would go crying to the house. (You know how little brothers are!)

This was in the days before automatic washers and more than two pairs of jeans. My mom would hang the little Levis on the line and tell him, "If you fall in one more time, you will get a licking!" (They had those in the olden days too.)

I couldn't wait to get back out to that ditch. I'd jump across and say, "Come on, Ronnie, you can do it. You only missed it by two inches last time!"

'Course he'd fall in and get in trouble and I would be glad, until I sat in church the next Sunday! Then I would feel terrible and promise God I'd be good—again.

It was a grand life, growing up in a family filled with love and good times. When I was fifteen, I told everyone I was going to Africa to be

a missionary. Whe·   ⁀ne I was going to
New York to be a·   enrolled at Montana
State College ʹ   .conomics. Now don't
laugh. I can't   ant me to sew you up an
outfit, I caʹ   vide the meals while I sew.
   But I ʔ   ʹhe year before I went to college, I   ᴄle didn't come riding up on a
horse

   My   a Sunday afternoon. I picked up a
girlfriᴄ.   ᴧn'. In Livingston there was one city
block that ʋ   and around and around . . . that is where
the gas shortage   ʹom a decade later. As we were driving
around we saw these ᴜ o guys in a car with MSC stickers in the back
window. I said, "Those are college guys! Let's get them to notice us!"
(Which clearly shows my priorities in those days.)

   They didn't seem to notice us. So I drove down a one-way alley the
wrong way, and we both leaned out the window and yelled—and
they noticed us!

   We said, "We will meet you at the morgue."

   Don't laugh. That is where the kids all met. If there wasn't a fu-
neral, there was always lots of parking!

   These two guys got out of their car and walked up to our car.
Leaning their elbows on the bottom of the open window, they
peered into the car and said, "How'd cha like to get in and ride
around with us?" (Where the inflection is in that statement depends
on whether you are hearing this story from me or him.)

   I said, "Oh no you don't. My parents are very strict. One of their
rules is I cannot ride around with strangers in their cars. But HOW'D
CHA LIKE TO GET IN AND RIDE AROUND WITH US??"

   And that is how I met my husband. We were married in Septem-
ber 1961 after my freshman year of college and his junior year. We
were so happy.

Phyllis: Up the "holler" on the south fork of Cherry River in Richwood, West Virginia, there's a little four-room house. That's where I was raised. I was child number four in a family of five girls. There were no boys, just girls. The first three girls, Billie, Betty and Joann, were two years apart. Then ten years later I was born. Five years later Linda joined the family.

Sometimes it was hard to figure out just where I fit in this fifteen-year span between Jo and Linda. If I wanted to go swimming with Joann I had to act grown up and behave myself or she wouldn't let me go! When I played with Linda, my younger sister, I had to put away my books and go get out the dolls. Sometimes we would go to the river to catch "crawdads." That was not my favorite thing to do, and usually by the time we were done it wasn't Linda's favorite either.

Do any of you have younger sisters? Do they ever bug you? Now I know I never bugged my older sisters, but Linda was a pro at it (and she still is). For instance, when I was young I liked to sit in the rocking chair with all of my books and read. Linda would come and hold me forward in the chair. I would push and push and then Linda would let go and I'd fly backward. Or she would let me rock a bit and then she'd hold me back. One day when being held forward, I got just a tad irritated and pushed back—hard.

A word of advice: don't set rocking chairs in front of windows. I flew back into that window and it made a loud noise. Then of course Linda got scared and made a loud noise. Mom showed up real quick and made some noise . . . and then I made a loud noise.

I sent Mom a copy of my talk one time and she wrote back and said, "Well, you did good. And I'm glad you're finally telling the truth about who pushed who through that window!"

When I was about six years old Mom and Dad got a divorce. The older girls were getting jobs or getting married and moving out. So for most of my growing up life, it was just me, my mom and Linda.

After Dad left, times were really rough for a number of reasons. For one thing, we didn't have much money. In fact, we didn't have any money! Mom wasn't in good health so she couldn't work outside the home. She tended her garden and canned the vegetables in the summer. During the long winter months she made the quilts for our beds.

Those winter nights were cold, as the wind whistled around the eves of the house and past the windowsills. I lay in my bed alone many nights shivering, waiting for my body heat to warm the cold sheets. Sometimes I would hear Linda and Mom talking and murmurs of laughter through the wall between our rooms. I knew Mom was cuddling Linda and warming her as they shared the same bed. At some point, jealousy and resentment slipped in through the cracks with the winter wind.

Sometimes before the winter was over the cellar was bare. I remember one time we had creamed tomatoes for breakfast, lunch and supper for several days. Mom used to laugh at the memory of the time Linda cried, "Mom, what say we just kill that old fat hen and have fried chicken?" It was a choice between the chicken for one meal or eggs for breakfasts.

Clothes were either handmade by Mom or hand-me-downs from neighbors or friends. Sometimes they came from the feed sacks Granny would have when she bought feed for her cow and chickens. One time in particular there was a gray piece with red and white hearts on it. Both Linda and I wanted it. So Mom did what any loving mother would do. Neither of us got a dress—but we both got blouses.

The little house had its own problems, even though Mom made sure it was clean. That window stayed broken with cardboard over it for quite a while. I remember a period of time when every pot and kettle in the house was placed around on the floor when it rained. The plinking drops made a nice sound though.

The nicest thing about the rain were the times Mom, Linda and I would go out and sit in the old porch swing during a rainstorm. We would take a quilt to wrap up in and swing, listen to the rain on the porch roof and sing along with the bullfrogs over in the swamp.

Every Sunday morning I would go to church with Aunt Edith. Sometimes Linda would go with us. Mom would never go. She said after the divorce she just didn't feel as welcome as she had before. So she stayed home and had lunch ready when we got home.

Every summer we would go to Aunt Viva's for a week. She lived about fifty miles away and we didn't get to see her very often. We always seemed to go when they had their "tent meetings." We would load up in Uncle Joe's old truck and go for the day and half the night. I think the preachers were louder then.

Uncle Burl, Mom's only brother, still lived at home with Granny and took care of the farm chores while Granny tended the "house stuff." He also worked as a logger.

Now, across the river from us was the railroad track. The log train would go up the river every morning before daylight. At the end of the day it would come back down, loaded with logs. Uncle Burl worked up the river. In the summer months, the river would get low, and he could cross on the rocks as a shortcut home. We would listen for the train to come down the river about 6 o'clock in the evening. If it sounded like it was slowing down, that meant Uncle Burl would swing down from the train and come across. Linda and I would run to the riverbank and watch as his long, lanky legs stretched from one dry rock to another.

As he came up on the shore, we waited with anticipation to see what he had for us. He always saved something from his lunch for us "young-uns." Sometimes it was half an egg sandwich, sometimes a boiled egg. The best times were when he would save a part of his lunch cake for us. No matter what it was, it was special because he remembered us.

He said later, "You young-uns don't know how many times I was so hungry and wanted to finish all my lunch. But I'd see two little heads waiting on the riverbank for me, and I'd put something back to save."

But the very best memories were the times Mom would get out her guitar and play those old songs for us. Some were gospel songs, some were ballads we never heard except when Mom sang them. Linda and I learned to sing along and always begged for "just one more song."

I didn't know how important money was until a few years later when I wanted some of the things that the other kids at school had—like hula hoops and a Ben Casey shirt. I really wanted one of those shirts! And kids can be so cruel when someone doesn't follow the norm. (I finally got one of those shirts after they went out of style.) I couldn't go to all the ball games and activities, so I went to the library. The library was free and I read everything I could get my hands on—Hardy Boys, Nancy Drew, Cherry Ames, Bobsey Twins, Zane Grey books and many more.

Life was not easy in those young years. There are some very painful memories, but there are also some very good ones.

At age sixteen I got married. All I can say is I must have been reading the wrong books!

3

To Thee Do I Pledge My Troth (Whatever That Is)

Lois: Robert and I learned about surviving on deer meat, beans and donations from relatives. After college, we moved to Great Falls where Robert got a job with the Montana Power Company. I got a job as Cascade County Extension Agent (in sewing, not foods). We had one son, Todd, born in Bozeman and three years later our second son, Kevin, was born in Great Falls.

I was still being good. We went to church on Sundays. I quoted all those Bible verses I had memorized in Sunday school years before. I told the people that my mom and dad were Christians, my grandparents were Christians and my great-aunt Ruth was one of the first missionaries in the Philippines. We were in. I was helping in the church nursery and was in charge of Vacation Bible School. Robert was transferred to Billings and our third son, Ross, was born there. We had a nice house in a nice neighborhood.

And we were attending a nice church. It was close to our house. They were glad to hear about my great-aunt Ruth. As soon as we arrived I told them my folks were Christians, my grandparents . . . my great-aunt Ruth. . . .

That year I was in charge of Vacation Bible School at the church. Within two weeks of moving to Billings and finding a church home, I was visited by two ladies from that church. One of the ladies invited me to attend their local Christian Women's Club (CWC) meeting and give a special feature on sewing.

I had never heard of the group. They said it was held at the Lake Hills Country Club. I thought it was probably a nice place for a nice person like me to go to, so I said, "Yes." The luncheon was nice, the people were nice, the decorations were nice and I thought the special feature was excellent! So when it came time to fill out their little yellow guest slip, I noticed a box at the bottom where it said, "Check if you would like to help in any way you can." I checked the box. The next month I was the new decorations chairman of Billings Christian Women's Club. Nice, huh?

A perfect life. I still couldn't cook. I wasn't athletic. But I went to church and I was very nice.

The things that were really important to me were looking good and being good. However, at this time in my life, this nice church lady got to doing some serious thinking. And watching and listening. I started watching the women at CWC, the speakers, the other gals on the committee and the women in my church. Their lives were not shallow. Looking good was not at the top of their lists. I started listening to Christian radio and the speakers on it. I start listening, really listening, to the sermons at my church. I started thinking about some of those Bible verses that I had memorized years before. And I started reading and studying my Bible—for me.

I saw myself still as that twelve-year-old girl, trying to be good enough for God. Only now it wasn't my little brother that was tripping me up, it was just life.

No—it was not life, it was me. Trying to be good enough for God. I was building a little house on my prairie all right. But I was doing it myself, brick by brick: a brick of daily Vacation Bible School, a brick of nursery duty, a brick of CWC, even a brick of baked beans to the potluck suppers now and then.

I had memorized a verse years ago that said, "For no one can lay any foundation other than the one already laid, which is Jesus Christ" (1 Corinthians 3:11). I could stack all the bricks I wanted on my dirt for my little house. But those good-works bricks wouldn't do. God's Word said (and I had memorized this one too, from Ephesians 2:8-9, KJV), "For by grace are ye saved through faith; and that not of yourselves: it is the gift of God: not of works [i.e., VBS, CWC, church, etc]." Right there I saw myself, trying to be good enough for God. The Bible also says, "All have sinned and fall short of the glory of God" (Romans 3:23). Even church ladies.

Then I made a realization. God had a blueprint for me. In fact, He has a plan for all of us. John 3:16 (KJV) says, "For God so loved the world, that he gave his only begotten Son, that whosoever believeth in him should not perish, but have everlasting life." We read it on our Christmas cards: "For unto you is born this day in the city of David a Saviour, which is Christ the Lord" (Luke 2:11, KJV). Why would He send His Son, Jesus Christ, if we didn't need saving?

That day I surrendered my life to God. I saw my sin and my need to be saved. I knelt beside my bed. I said through tears, "Forgive me for trying to do it my way. Jesus, come into my life. Forgive my sins. You be in charge. I will follow Your building plans from now on believing that You are who You say You are and that Your Word applies to me." I think from my former cowgirl days I said, "I am turning the reins over to You."

My life is different because of that day. He has changed and blessed the direction of my life. When I got up from my knees, I still couldn't cook. I still wasn't athletic. But my foundation was different. I was on a different path with my life. By God's grace and mercy I could walk in faith with Him. Church became so much more meaningful because it wasn't about "perfect" me anymore . . . but about Him.

After we had been in Billings, Montana for three years we heard about the Colstrip steam-generating plant project. Robert and I both wanted to go. We started praying and asked our friends to pray for us. It sounded like a marvelous adventure. We prayed to get to go to Colstrip, Montana.

Phyllis: Of course I knew what I wanted when I got married at sixteen! Doesn't every sixteen-year-old? I think what I really wanted was for someone to say, "No, Phyllis, you're not getting married. You're too young!" The ones who did say it were too busy with their own lives to enforce it, but they made the halfhearted effort.

Mom sent me to see Daddy, and he said it was up to Mom. Mom said she didn't think I should, but it was up to me. She did the laundry while I went downtown to get married.

The old saying is "You've made your bed, now lie in it!" I was determined to make this marriage work, so I was going to do everything I could to make it do so. I was going to prove that I could be the best wife. (After all, you know what those older sisters would have said.) So I apologized for every fight or argument, regardless of who was to blame.

Granny used to say, "Pride makes an ugly bedfellow."

I was also going to be the best mom. Kevin was born when I was seventeen and Kelly was born on my nineteenth birthday. I now had two sons. I had read somewhere that flannel pajamas were good, so I had Mom make them two pair each. After their bath I parted their hair and put them in their new pj's. I shook baby powder all over them, 'cause I'd read that was good too. They were so cute it almost made me forget everything they had done all day!

And I was going to be the best housekeeper. (You know what people would have said!) I even planned out a cleaning schedule. For example, on Thursdays I did baseboards and windows throughout the house. Sometimes when Mom would go to the store she would stop by my house and visit for a minute or have a cup of coffee.

One day I asked her in and she said, "Oh no, Phyllis, I don't want to come in. I might mess up your house."

"How can you mess up the house, Mom? We're just going to have coffee!"

She answered, "Well, you know, I just don't like to visit you. I'm always afraid I'll mess things up, and everything is always in its place and looks so perfect. It just looks cold."

Well now, that certainly gave me a "warm fuzzy" right in the middle of my stomach! (But I'll have you know that Mom came to visit me a few years ago and found one of the warmest houses in Montana!)

I was trying to measure up to what I thought everyone expected of me. What I didn't let anyone know back then was that it was an abusive marriage. I just stayed away from everyone when it was bad. One day I didn't open the door for Mom when she came by because I didn't want her to see my face or the bruises on my body. Pride and fear became buddies.

Along about this time my sister Betty died. She was the one who had taught me how to fix my hair and gave me my first "perm." She was the one who taught me how to do my nails. She was the one who bought me an old bike when I wanted one so much and helped me paint it blue and white. She even let me pick the colors. She was the one who gave me her new Easter dress so I could have a nice dress to be married in. Now she was dead at thirty-five years old. I didn't think I liked God much anymore.

Then Fred and I moved from West Virginia to Butte, Montana, and it became much easier to hide the abuse. The house was filled with slamming doors and angry words. The boys were growing up in this home and coping the best they knew how. By their teenage years, Kevin had a drinking problem and Kelly was into drugs. They had traded flannel pj's for black leather, long hair and beards. Kelly wore Levi jackets with ugly pictures on the back. They were out of the house and out of school most of the time. They were into jails, treatment centers, emergency rooms and anything else they could find to get into! It wasn't unusual for the telephone to ring at all hours of the night. A full night of sleep was unheard of.

I was coping too. I was using—mostly abusing—prescription drugs and drinking. Once, I "overcoped" and ended up in the hospital. I was just so tired! I had tried so hard at everything, and everything had failed. I would hear about the neighbor's kids and their accomplishments and I'd think, *Are they better parents than I am? Maybe I'm not trying hard enough. Maybe I'm not doing something right. Why is everything such a mess when I've tried so hard?*

At the end of sixteen years, I got tired of trying and bailed out. I just did what I used to do when I went swimming with Jo—I just held my nose and jumped! I got a job that paid $3.47 an hour and moved into a trailer with a bed and a chair. I just wanted peace. The cute little house didn't matter. The "I'm sorrys" hadn't done any good. And who knew where the boys were or what they were up to? I was mad at the world. I was even mad at the neighbor lady because her kid was off to college and her life was rosy. Bitterness was making itself at home.

After the divorce I married Jim. I had known him a long time and I thought he was a nice guy (and I still do). The boys weren't happy about Jim changing from their buddy to an authority figure in their life so there was an adjustment period. They "adjusted" each other rather frequently. As the boys got older they moved out on their own. Kevin went into the Marines and Kelly graduated (finally!) and was working as a radio DJ.

Jim was laid off from construction again and ended up with a full-time job in Colstrip, Montana, the one town we had vowed we would never move to! I did not pray to go to Colstrip, Montana!

4

Colstrip: The Marvelous Adventure?

Lois: Robert and I just loved Colstrip! The town had been built in 1923 so that coal could be mined for use in the Northern Pacific Railroad locomotives. When that need diminished, so did the town. However, when a coal-fired steam-generating plant was built in Billings, the coal of Colstrip was needed once again. In 1972 the construction of coal-fired steam-generating plants was begun in Colstrip. The city became a boomtown once more. This was the project we had prayed to be part of. The town grew from 200 to 8,500 in a few years. Everything from schools to stores to streets and houses had to be built. We felt like modern-day pioneers. So many things were new. We were charter members of everything. We loved the adventure of it all. Todd, Kevin and Ross formed friendships quickly. They were in many school activities.

We were living in an apartment while waiting for our home to be built. One day I looked out the window and saw a guy wearing a green hard hat with a Christian "fish" sign on it. I asked if he was a Christian. He said, "Yes, I am. So is my wife."

"Hallelujah!" I said. We hadn't met any Christians yet.

We began going to a Bible study together. From there a church was formed. It began in a home and then moved to the old mess hall. Rev. Henry Babis from Chicago was called as our first pastor. We moved our church to a mobile trailer and a few years later we were able to build a church building of our own.

We started Bible studies for women. God brought many folks into His family through those studies. Our church fellowship at the Colstrip Alliance Church was close and encouraging. What a joy to be in a growing church family. The years seemed to race by as the Lord blessed our life in Colstrip. Our children grew as fast as our town! They had been little boys when we moved to Colstrip. Now they were young men.

Our youngest son, Ross, was in a major vehicle accident in his junior year of high school. It was a very tragic event. One man died and a woman was left in very serious condition. Because the left turn signal was in the on position when they pried the car and our truck (which he had been driving) apart, the accident became our responsibility. Our son was not yet eighteen. Everything from court hearings, insurance nightmares, claims, lawsuits and legal proceedings followed. In one instant, the life of our son and that of our family changed.

How did this fit into the Bible promise that "all things work together for good to them that love God, to them who are the called according to his purpose" (Romans 8:28, KJV)? The tragedy that took a man's life and altered his family forever was impossible to understand. The woman who was injured in the accident would never know life as it was before. The fallout from the accident turned our home into a battle zone. How could those families survive? How would we survive? So many lives changed in one instant.

After several bad experiences with well-meaning counselors, we were told by dear friends to find a Christian counselor. "You need someone who has a belief system the same as yours," they said.

We had had no experience in family problems up to this point, so we didn't know anything about all this stuff. We just knew we were a family in big trouble. There were harassing phone calls in the middle of the night. Our son went through a horrible time—we all did. We could not understand ourselves or our own feelings as we dealt with all of this, let alone try to understand each other.

We found a Christian psychologist who would take our case in Billings, 130 miles away. We drove the 260-mile round trip for counseling with him one night a week for over a year. I reminded God of the verse that He would not tempt us beyond what we are able to handle. I told God that He was wrong—this was too much. I could not handle what He had allowed.

I prayed and cried and prayed and cried for months. God was true to His promise that He would never leave us or forsake us. When we look back on that time now, we see God's hand of protection upon us as we learned to walk "through the fire and floods."

There were people at church who constantly stood by us and prayed for us. Our son's Sunday school teachers came to our home and stepped up to the challenge time and time again. Ladies from churches and retreats where I had been a speaker prayed continually.

A year later, we could sense God's precious hand of healing taking over. God had been working in our family. I knew there was a long way to go but we were on the right path, together. The psychologist said that I needed to do something for myself at this time. "Sign up for a class, find a new hobby, do something to get out of the house," he said.

I had always wanted one of those ceramic nativity scenes to set out at Christmas. I looked up the address of a local ceramic shop. I decided to go there. I could do ceramics.

 Phyllis: Jim and I pulled into Colstrip about midnight (pretty appropriate). We had found a house, left one boy with his job and the other with Uncle Sam in Butte, and taken the dog. (He was a good dog.) Everything started to settle—on the surface. There was a measure of peace coming into my life. Jim had a steady job with no "pink slip" coming every few weeks, the house was cute and the dog was still behaving. We were only getting the highlights of what was going on with the boys. So life was quieting down.

But I realized something—I was still angry! I was still bitter! The unwanted houseguests of pride and fear had moved right along with us. I couldn't blame it on my kids or my ex-husband because they were away. Now who was to blame? Now what? I had to start looking at Phyllis and I didn't like what I saw.

Remember Linda, that little sister of mine? She had grown up and had some problems of her own. She did something about it. She got religion. I told Linda, "Don't try to shove it down my throat. If it works for you, that's good, but I don't want any part of it!" I had an emergency room God. When things got too bad, I'd cry out to Him—"Help!" Then when the crisis was over, I would forget about Him and hope He would forget about me.

You see, I knew there were some things in my life God probably didn't like. He probably didn't like my attitude. I was so tired of trying to please everyone and worrying about what they thought that I just jumped to the other side of the fence. I decided I didn't care if I pleased anyone! So I did what I wanted, said what I wanted and if people didn't like it—tough. I had turned into a real sweetheart over the years.

I was also pretty sure God didn't like my mouth. Because of all the anger and bitterness within me, I had no way to release it except through my words. So I "cussed" with every breath. (Someone asked me one time if I shouldn't say "cursing." I don't care what you call it—it all sounds the same.) And I could not stop! The more I tried, the worse it got! My sister Billie said, "If God doesn't do anything else with Phyllis Jean, I hope He cleans up her mouth!"

I didn't even want to try to make changes in my life. After all, everything I had tried had failed. I certainly wasn't going to tackle God and have Him mad at me! He probably wanted me to trade in my jeans and shorts for dresses and would make me grow long hair. I wasn't ready to give them up. I figured if I couldn't please people and do what they expected of me, how on earth was I ever going to please God? I didn't know at that time that it was probably a whole lot easier to please one God who loved me than a bunch of people who didn't.

So for ten years, Linda prayed. She would talk to me when I went home on vacation. She sent me all those little cards with butterflies and rainbows. I didn't pay any attention to them. I used them as coasters to set my coffee cups on and never looked up any of those verses. Linda must have figured that out because she started writing those verses out.

But I still never paid any attention. I would just keep telling her to keep her Jesus to herself. I said, "Linda, I can't live it and I'm not even going to try." But oh, how I wanted to believe her! How I wanted to believe there was something worth living for in this life! Surely there was something besides this emptiness! Part of me wanted so badly to step out and see if I could do it. But every time I had trusted someone it had just brought more hurt and disappointment. I was just too tired and too scared.

Things were still happening in the lives of my sons and I worried about them constantly. The year after we moved to Colstrip, Kevin was injured in an accident. He was hospitalized in intensive care for several days following emergency surgery to repair a ruptured spleen. He also had a collapsed lung. The doctor wasn't sure he was going to make it. I felt so helpless as Jim and I stood at the hospital window waiting for word to come. There was another family in the room with me. They waited for word of their father and husband who was in surgery. In the midst of their own worries they saw mine and asked, "Would you like us to call the prayer chain in our church and have them pray for your son?"

I knew anything God had to offer at this point was more than I had. "Please do," I said.

Kelly was in Butte with his heavy-metal band, and I knew drugs were a big part of his life. I held my breath every time the telephone rang. He was so angry! Sometimes when I talked to him on the phone he would tell me of the horrible nightmares he was having. Even then I knew God was the answer, but every time I mentioned Him, Kelly would grit his teeth and say, "Don't even talk to me about God!" And yet I could hear my little boy in flannel pajamas beneath all the turmoil. How I wished I knew how to help him.

Linda just talked to me and prayed. Then one day she called from Ohio, saying, "Phyllis, guess what! We're coming to Montana on our vacation this year!"

I said, "Well, that's great! How long do you get to stay?"

She answered, "Two weeks!"

I said, "You mean you have a few days to drive out, visit and then drive back?"

"Oh no," she trilled in my ear, "Rick has a month! We are taking a week to drive out, two weeks with you and a week to drive back."

She was coming to stay for two weeks! I told her there wasn't a lot to do in Colstrip. She said that was OK because she was just coming to see me.

I hung up the phone and told Jim that we had to take them camping. I couldn't stand to have Linda in the house for two weeks, preaching. So we decided to take them up in the mountains south of Butte, Montana. I used to hunt up there with Jim and I knew those mountains . . . and Linda didn't.

July came, and so did Linda and Rick.

Linda had a camcorder and a camera, and she was taking pictures of everything. She saw cowboys by the fence and thought I had told them to go out and act like cowboys. She had taken pictures of deer, antelope and cactus blooming by the fence post. She said she had taken a picture of a porcupine in South Dakota, and people had laughed at her. I didn't know why they would have laughed—until Rick told me it was roadkill.

So we took them to the mountains to camp and it was the best thing we could have done. She was preoccupied. Did I mention that she talked weird? "Thank You, Lord, for the bologna sandwich and the beautiful sunset . . ." and on and on.

One morning after breakfast she said, "Phyllis, grab your coffee and let's go see if we can get a picture of an elk." I explained that it wasn't always an easy thing to do, but she was persistent. So I did the only thing I could do—I grabbed my coffee.

We walked down the road for fifteen or twenty minutes and she pointed to a field and exclaimed, "What's that?" I looked and said it must be some kind of birds. Well, in a few seconds that field of "birds" turned into the ears on a whole herd of elk as they stood up. They let her take their picture and then walked off into the timber.

Have you ever hunted elk? Have they ever just stood up in the field right in front of you? They did for Linda. And she got a picture.

Then it was the last night. We were riding four in the cab of the pickup and she was thanking the Lord for it all, and then she added, "But Lord, I'd really like to see a bear and a moose before I leave."

I thought, *Well, of course you would.* Five minutes later, in the middle of the road, there stood two moose, just waiting. Linda grabbed her camera and started doing her thing. And I started believing.

I got to see Linda in an everyday relationship with her Lord Jesus Christ. And she was liking it. It wasn't a chore or something that she had to do. I said, "You act like He's your best friend or something."

And she replied that He was. She told me that He had said, "I will never leave you or forsake you."

Linda went on back to Ohio, and I started thinking about this new side of God—Someone who loved you and was always with you. Not Someone who was going to "get you" when you did something wrong.

I had started going to the ceramic shop across the street and helping out. This lady walked in one day and said, "Hi, I'm Lois Olmstead and I want to make one of those ceramic nativity sets, the biggest one you've got."

I thought, *Well, well.* And said, "How would you like to do that?"

She said, "Could you show me some examples of the procedures?"

So I showed her glazed. She didn't like glazed; it was too plain. Did she like just painting? No. Chalking? Yes, she liked chalking. She liked the procedure that takes forever, and she had twenty-six pieces to do in two weeks. I was not impressed.

Everyone in town knew her, and I had heard about her and her family crisis. In my bitterness I had no sympathy for her. Now she was going to see how the rest of the world lived. She would see how everyone else deals with life when it's not all sunshine and roses. Anyone can smile when life is good.

I knew she was one of those "holier-than-thous." I knew she went to church somewhere there in town. She was always talking about it and the new church building they were working on. Some other ladies started coming from that church. They all talked about potlucks and Sunday school. They would discuss a Bible study or something the pastor had said.

And they were having fun! They sounded like Linda. I listened. (But I didn't let them know I was listening.) And I watched. (I already sensed I was becoming their "project.") So this was how the religious people lived and acted outside the church doors.

I didn't change when they walked in that ceramic shop door. I still talked the way I would normally talk and if they didn't like it that was tough! For six months I watched and listened and I told Linda about them. She thought that was wonderful.

Linda would quote Scripture to me: "John 3:16 says, 'For God so loved the world, that he gave his only begotten Son, that whosoever believeth in him should not perish, but have everlasting life' " (KJV).

I said, "I know that verse. I memorized it when I was little and going to church with Aunt Edith."

She said, "But Phyllis, *He so loved.*"

I didn't think there was a whole lot about me to love and wondered what that had to do with me. When that thought wasn't running through my mind, I would argue that I was as good as any of those hypocrites singing in church on Sunday morning.

But Linda was persistent. She said, "It doesn't matter who you are or what you've done, Phyllis. What matters is what Jesus Christ, the Son of God, did on that cross for you."

I said, "That was 2,000 years ago, not today."

She said there was a verse in Hebrews (10:12) that tells us that He was the one final sacrifice for all sins, forever—for whosoever would believe.

All sin? Forever? I figured I must be in there somewhere, and I figured there were probably a couple of sins I could confess.

After a few months I started thinking about going to church. I hadn't been inside one for almost twenty years. I decided to go where these ladies attended, since they were the only church people I knew.

I asked Linda if this church was all right, and she said, "Sure it is. I asked my pastor and he said they were good people who preached the Word of God."

So on Saturday night I lay there thinking about all the important decisions facing me. Like—what was I going to wear? I tossed and turned and turned and tossed. Jim finally said, "Phyllis, I have to get up at 5 o'clock and go to work. So either lie still or move!"

So I moved out to the couch and continued listening to all those thoughts running through my head. *What if I don't know where to go or what door to go in? What if I get stuck in the parking lot? What if I don't know where to go when I get in there? They'll say, "What's she doing in the broom closet?"*

After every thought there was a line of an old gospel song Mom used to sing that would run through my mind like an answer: "Where could I go but to the Lord?"

At 4 o'clock the clock chimed and I decided I wasn't going to go. And I went to sleep. At 8 o'clock I woke up. I had forgotten that when it's 8 o'clock in Montana it's 10 o'clock in Ohio, and Linda had the whole Sunday school praying that I would get up and go to church.

I wore my pantsuit. I got there and sat in the car and waited. There was nobody else going in. I was not going to walk in by myself! But I was up and there and dressed. I told myself just to get out and go in. I got out of the car and walked up that long parking lot. A long arm reached out and dragged me in. (Now that parking lot has shrunk, but the arm is still the same.) It was the arm of the head usher, Robert Olmstead, and he's six feet nine inches tall.

He said, "Good morning, I'm glad you're here." I told him good morning but didn't say I was glad to be there. He sent me to have a seat and said Lois would be up to sit with me in a minute.

I sat in the middle. (I found out later that the back row is reserved for the regulars.)

Lois came up and sat with me and that was nice. The pastor's wife came over and introduced herself and that was nice. Some people sitting behind me introduced themselves and that was nice. Then they all went away and left me alone and I really thought that was nice. I told myself, *Only an hour. You can do anything for an hour and then you can just go home.*

They sang the first song and I kind of remembered it and hummed along. Then they sang a chorus, and I had to sit and listen. It was about why Christ died on Calvary—to restore broken lives and to heal broken hearts.

I started to cry. I cried and cried. I started digging in the bottom of my purse, but I couldn't find a tissue.

Lois started looking through her purse, and she didn't have one either. She got down to the bottom of her purse where the pennies and lint are and found a Certs. She handed that to me and said, "Will this help?"

I sat and chewed on that mint and cried. (She said later that she'd never seen anybody cry when the offering basket went by.)

I went home that day and I felt so good. I felt like a weight had been lifted and all I'd done was go to church, and millions of people do that every Sunday. Something had changed on the inside of me.

The Bible says God knows your heart. I guess He knew I was ready to give up my jeans and shorts. He knew I was ready to wear dresses all the time and let my hair grow out if that's what it took. (After all, I was over forty, so it was time to settle down.) I walked in that door that Sunday ready to lay down all I thought He wanted.

I have since read somewhere that we should make a list of everything we thought God wanted of us and put the hardest one to give up on the top of the list. And if we'd give Him that one, He'd have all the rest. If I had known He wanted what was on the inside, I may not have walked in those doors. It would have seemed too hopeless.

I clearly remember walking outside the next morning, looking up at the blue sky and saying, "Good morning, Lord!" My tulips were in bloom.

On Tuesday night Linda called. (I'm not sure how she waited till Tuesday.) We talked a little and she finally asked about church.

I told her it was awful.

She said, "What happened? Weren't the people nice to you?"

I told her they were all very nice.

She said, "Well, didn't you like the pastor?" (Have I mentioned she's persistent?)

I assured her the pastor and his wife were both very nice.

"Well then, what's wrong?" she exclaimed in frustration.

I told her that I'd cried all the way through it.

She laughed and said, "Oh, Phyllis, He is going to get you." I knew she wasn't talking about the pastor. She asked if I had "prayed the prayer."

I said that I hadn't. I'd gone to church. I liked it. I'd probably go back and I wasn't cussing anymore. What more did she want? After two hours she commented that she hadn't heard one cuss word. That was really good, but she insisted that I needed to "pray the prayer." She said, "Phyllis, I hear something different in your voice. I really believe God has touched you and done a work in you. But things might happen down the road. Life might get rough." (I don't know what she thought they'd been before!) "The devil will come and say, 'Nothing happened to you. All you did was go to church—do you think that's going to make a difference?' " She said I needed to make the decision so that I would know that I know that I had turned my life over to God.

I told her I would think about it.

Linda had told me that First John 1:9 says, "If we confess our sins, he is faithful and just to forgive us our sins, and to cleanse us from all unrighteousness" (KJV). Well, I knew a little bit about cleaning. (Remember that schedule?) And for a while I cleaned houses for people in Colstrip. They would say, "You know, Phyllis, with all the kids and my working, I just can't seem to get caught up on things. Will you come in and clean for me? Here's the key to my house."

I would go and begin to clean through the house. In the living room I could just take that spray can and psssst! that table would just shine! As I finished in the living room, I would move on to the kitchen, bath, hallways and bedrooms. Cleaning, spraying, wiping—sometimes scrubbing if the stain had been there a while. Room by room—piece by piece until the whole house was clean.

That's how Jesus would come in and cleanse me? Cleanse me from the anger? The bitterness? The resentment? A hurt hidden deep in the closet at the end of the hall, brought out and healed? All those things that had crept in during the years? Jesus wanted to cleanse me of all that? Is that what Jesus did with the cussing—to show me what He could do if I were to turn my whole life over to Him? I didn't have to be "instantly perfect"?

I thought about it, and a little later I went in and knelt by my bed. I told God that I wasn't going to be a halfway Christian. If I was going to do this I was going to do it right. I told him that I needed His help because I couldn't do it by myself. (I think He already knew that.) I asked Jesus Christ "to forgive me of all my sin, come into my life and cleanse me. Amen."

The cleansing and scrubbing had begun.

I went to church on Wednesday night. (I found out I could go then too, it wasn't just for all those spiritual people.)

My friend Lois came in and asked if I had made the coffee. I replied that I hadn't made the coffee but I had made the decision. She hugged me and she cried . . . and she still didn't have any tissues.

Lois: Do you know the Lord? You can come from up a creek or down a holler. You can be really good and know all those Bible verses. You could come from a home where you didn't feel loved. You could have done all kinds of things that you regret. God says in His Word that if we confess our sins, He will forgive us our sins and cleanse us from all unrighteousness.

> Thank You, Lord, for a brand-new day
> All my sins have been washed away
> Forgiveness is flowing
> Faith is now growing
> Because Jesus has now come to stay.

> Phyllis Rowe © 2000

God loves you. He wants to forgive you of your sins. He says if we believe in our heart and we confess with our mouth, we shall be saved (Romans 10:9). We want to give you that opportunity right now.

Please take a moment to read these verses. Then if you would like to surrender your life to Jesus on this day, just write your prayer on the lines provided, sign your name and write the date on the space provided. Just as Phyllis said: it will be a reminder to you, if doubts come, that today you did ask God to forgive your sins, and He came into your life. He does what His Word says He will do.

Jesus answered, "I am the way and the truth and the life. No one comes to the Father except through me." (John 14:6)

For all have sinned and fall short of the glory of God. (Romans 3:23)

For the wages of sin is death, but the gift of God is eternal life in Christ Jesus our Lord. (Romans 6:23)

For it is by grace you have been saved, through faith—and this not from yourselves, it is the gift of God— not by works, so that no one can boast. (Ephesians 2:8-9)

If you confess with your mouth, "Jesus is Lord," and believe in your heart that God raised him from the dead, you will be saved. For it is with your heart that you believe and are justified, and it is with your mouth that you confess and are saved. (Romans 10:9-10)

If we confess our sins, he is faithful and just and will forgive us our sins and purify us from all unrighteousness. (1 John 1:9)

Prayer: *Dear God, I know I am a sinner. I believe that Jesus died to forgive me of my sins. Please forgive me of my sins and live in my heart. Thank You for forgiving me of all my sins. Thank You for giving me new life, eternal life. From this moment forward, I will choose to follow You.*

Your Prayer _____

_____

_____

_____

_____

Your Name _____

Date _____

Psalm 100

Make a joyful noise unto the LORD, *all ye lands.*
Serve the LORD *with gladness: come before His presence*
    with singing.
Know ye that the LORD *he is God:*
It is he that hath made us, and not we ourselves;
we are his people, and the sheep of his pasture.
Enter into his gates with thanksgiving, and into his courts
    with praise:
be thankful unto him, and bless his name.
For the LORD *is good;*
his mercy is everlasting; and his truth endureth to all
    generations. (KJV)

5

In the Pew

Phyllis: Well, here we were. We were in the same church. Shortly after we started attending the Christian and Missionary Alliance church, Pastor Shaefer baptized Jim and me in Castle Rock Lake (locally known as "the surge pond"). I wanted to "do it right," you know. As soon as we heard about "membership," we wanted to do that too. So we did. We were getting involved.

Lois and I started traveling and doing things together. She'd ask if I wanted to go with her, and Jim would say, "Go." So we'd go and talk . . . and talk . . . and talk. And drink coffee. This was a whole new world for me. I was learning new phrases like "hallelujah," "Praise the Lord," "fellowship" (what's fellowship?), "sanctification" (what's that!?), "consecration"—and on and on and on. I would say these words sometimes and then think, *Did I say that?* It was like learning a whole new language. I sometimes felt like I was visiting a foreign land right in my own backyard.

I remember my first trip to the Christian bookstore. I didn't even know there was such a thing! The store had all these crosses and rainbows and butterflies. (Now I know where Linda got them.) And books and music. They even had Christian music in the style I liked.

I found out Lois could be fun (for a religious person) and meeting all the other people was great.

I can't explain what a turnaround that was in my life. It was like night and day! For the first time, there was hope in my life. I was not depending on something I could do, but depending on what *God* could do. I had something to look forward to each day. And besides—if God could change me, maybe He could change my boys. They may have been rotten, but I loved them. It was exciting! And I was learning.

One of the first things God started teaching me was the power of prayer. Jeremiah 33:3 says, "Call unto me, and I will answer thee, and show thee great and mighty things, which thou knowest not" (KJV).

About two weeks after I turned my life over to the Lord, Kevin was off on a drinking binge. I went to bed at twenty minutes until midnight and lay there in bed wondering where he was, and if he was all right. I began to pray.

Suddenly, I found myself praying exactly what I wanted God to do with Kevin. I prayed, "Lord, wherever Kevin is right now, will You just reach down and touch him? Will You open his eyes and let him see what the drinking is doing to his life? Will You open his ears and let him hear all the things that are said to him about You? Lord, will You just touch him right now? Only You know exactly where he is and what he is doing. Only You can do anything to change all this. Will You touch him, Lord?"

As the clock struck midnight, the telephone rang. My heart thudded in the familiar fear. Kevin was on the other end. He was crying and the first words he said were, "Mom, I need help. My life is a mess."

Well, this was no revelation to me, but I wondered what made him realize it. I asked him and his response was, "Mom, I was just walking down the street here in Billings, minding my own business.

Drunk but happy. All of a sudden, Mom, I just began to shake and started crying! Mom, my life is a mess!"

We talked, and he eventually made it home. Did God change him that night? No. Did he stop drinking that night? No. What did happen is God got my attention. When we pray—He hears. The answer is coming. We just don't know when.

One month after I had turned my life over to Jesus Christ, Jim had too. I guess he liked the difference he saw. Kelly came from Butte to visit and said he saw something in my face he'd never seen before, and if it was real, he wanted it too! He "prayed the prayer." A year later Kevin asked Jesus to forgive him and come into his life as well!

I found a verse in the Bible that said, "Commit your way to the LORD, trust also in Him, and He shall bring it to pass" (Psalm 37:5, NKJV). I started thinking about some things I wanted to commit into His hands.

Shortly after Kelly asked Jesus to be his Savior, he ended up down in California, still with his heavy-metal band. Was he perfect? No. (The cleaning process had only begun.) After a few months he called and said the drugs were getting the best of him. He was out of control. He was scared. He said, "Mom, will you and your friends pray that I can kick this stuff and get out of here? I know what the treatment centers say to do, and I can do that, but I just know God can help me more."

I told him we would pray.

Several months later he called and said, "Mom, you said Aunt Billie is sending me some money. We have a chance to rent a warehouse here for the band and my share is $450. If that is what she sends, then I'll know I'm to stay. If not, then I guess I'll have my answer."

I called to talk to Billie and found out she was upset. "I wanted to send Kelly $450, but as it worked out, I only have $300 to send him," she said. (This is the only time she ever sent money to one of my boys!) I reassured her that the $300 was fine.

The day came for Kelly to head home with the $300 God sent him (through Billie). He had the car loaded and stopped for a soft drink to go with his sandwiches. He also needed a Styrofoam cooler to hold them. As he looked on the shelf at the coolers, he laid his wallet down. It had all of his money in it. When he got to the counter, he missed the wallet. Of course when he went back to the shelf, it was gone.

He was so angry! He was so close to leaving and heading for home and now there was another snag to hold him. He went out to the parking lot and slammed his fist into a power pole. He said later, "I knew I would still get home. I just didn't know how."

As he stood there, he heard a gruff voice call to him, "Hey, buddy!"

Kelly turned around to see a man walking across the parking lot toward him. In his outstretched hand was Kelly's missing wallet. With all the money intact.

"I'm sorry," he said.

"It's all right." Kelly answered.

Kelly made it home, and God continued scrubbing. We talked . . . and talked . . . and talked. I didn't know very much about all this church stuff and Jesus, but I guess you only have to know one step more than the person you're talking to.

Anyway, Kelly listened and learned and healed. Pastor Schaefer baptized him in the city pool on a cool, windy day.

We were wondering what the next step would be about six weeks later, when Fred, my ex-husband, called from Elko, Nevada. He said he could get Kelly a job down there with him. So Kelly packed up his little green car and headed off in the new direction the Lord had given him.

God was revealing Himself to me in ways I could only dream of. Did that mean there would be no more problems? No. It only meant now God was in charge. Now He could begin the cleansing in all of our lives. I wanted Jesus to be Lord of my life, and He was showing me that He truly is the Way, the Truth and the Life.

* * *

The Lord was doing so many good things in my life, and I was overwhelmed with His goodness. I knew things didn't always happen this fast for most people, and I was so grateful. As the Lord taught me the power of prayer, I decided to teach my granddaughter, Jaree, as well. She spent a lot of time with us, and one day she seemed unusually quiet. I asked if anything was wrong. I told her we could pray about it.

"No, Gramma. I'm just thinking about something. I'll just pray by myself when I get home."

"Well," I replied, "can we pray about it together? You know Jesus loves you, and He hears us when we pray. The Bible says, 'For where two or three are gathered together in My name, I am there in the midst of them' (Matthew 18:20, NKJV). You know Grampa and I would be glad to pray with you."

"No, Gramma, I'll just pray by myself when I get home."

"Well, honey," I insisted, "the Bible also says, 'if two of you agree on earth concerning anything that they ask, it will be done for them by My Father in heaven' (Matthew 18:19, NKJV). If you don't want Grampa to pray with us, would you like just you and me to pray?"

She sat solemnly and then asked, "Gramma, what does the Bible say about just one praying?"

I thought for a minute and answered, "Well, actually, it says, 'The effective, fervent prayer of a righteous man avails much' (James 5:16, NKJV)."

"I'll pray when I get home," she stated quietly.

"OK," I said.

Jaree's mom, Lisa, was also learning about the power of prayer. She was changing the oil in her car and came over to borrow Jim's oil filter wrench. A few hours later she walked in the door with a sheepish look on her face as she held up a mangled tool.

"What on earth did you do to my filter wrench?" Jim asked with a laugh.

She just grinned and answered, "Well, I couldn't get it loose, so I prayed for God to give me strength!"

God had been teaching me the first part of Psalm 37:5: "Commit your way to the LORD," as He taught me about prayer. Then He began teaching me the second part of the verse, "Trust also in Him" (NKJV).

Four months after I asked the Lord to take over in my life, Jim suddenly bent over with chest pain. At the time we happened to be in West Virginia on vacation. Like the loving wife I am, I told him he had just been eating too much of Mom's good cooking.

We went to a doctor and he said it was Jim's heart. Neither one of us could believe that, so we continued our vacation for two weeks. By the end of this time, we were getting scared. Whatever this was wasn't going away! We made it home only by God's protective hand, and the day after arriving home, Jim was in the Billings hospital having an angiogram and angioplasty done on his heart.

We sounded like Linda for a while as we thanked God for His goodness. Then six weeks later they took Jim to Billings again. This time they took him from work in an ambulance. They did the same procedure again. This time I wasn't too happy with God. I thought He was supposed to be in charge of things. Now remember, the boys were still "doing their thing" too. Sometimes the cleaning process takes time . . . especially if the stains have been there a while.

I went to the church and talked with Lois and Pastor Schaefer. They reassured me God was in control, that I just had to hold on and trust Him. It's awfully hard to trust someone you just met! So I blew my nose on cheap paper towels and decided there was nothing to go back to. I had to trust my newfound Savior.

It's a good thing I did, because six weeks later, Jim ended up back in the hospital. This time he had open-heart surgery and a double bypass. He was off work for two and one-half months. The bills went up and the paycheck went down. But God was in control of our lives now, and He showed His faithfulness in many, many ways.

The night Jim went into the hospital for the bypass surgery, the church had some special singers in from Billings. I went to listen and was comforted and blessed as they sang. (They sang my style of music.)

At the end of the evening, the pastor announced that there would be an offering taken. This was to help the group with their trip expenses. I looked in my purse and saw that I had $6—a $1 bill and a $5 bill. Jim was already in the hospital, and I knew I would be spending my next week in the hospital waiting room. I wanted to give something because I had been comforted as they sang the words of truth. I gave the dollar as the basket went by and tucked the $5 bill back in my purse carefully.

The next day I sat with Jim, waiting for the doctor to come in and tell us the plans for the surgery. Wayne from the church came in and sat down with us. In a few minutes he handed Jim an envelope and said, "This is for you."

Jim looked at the contents of the envelope, and then handed it to me to read. Wayne said, "When the people who sang last night heard there was a family with a medical need, they turned all the gas money they had received back over to us to give to you."

I looked down at the check in my hands. It was for $101. I wished I'd given the $5!

I was learning a lot from life situations and from God's people.

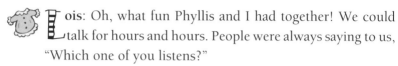**L**ois: Oh, what fun Phyllis and I had together! We could talk for hours and hours. People were always saying to us, "Which one of you listens?"

We'd answer, "It depends on the day! Sometimes we both talk and listen in between the commas!"

It blessed my socks off to see Phyllis growing in her devotion to our Lord. It was fun to have someone close to my age to do church stuff with and we were always thinking up something. There was a church building program going on. We both helped with that.

The Reminder

Lord, thank You for my special friend;
She's been a friendship treasure.
Her inspiration and steadfast faith
Is way beyond my measure.

Thank You, Lord, for our acceptance
Of each other in spite of our faults
And for the trust between us
Perhaps the nicest bond of all.

Would You gently touch her
When my friend is feeling low?
'Cause if she needs a special blessing,
You'll be the first to know.

And Lord, when she has a bad day,
And needs a friend or two,
Would You just remind me to pray,
And lift her up to You?

(A gift to Lois from Phyllis, Christmas 1987) Phyllis Rowe © 1987

And that first year, I finally got the ceramic set done! Not in three weeks, but in six months. In May, I had a Christmas party at our home. I put up a tree and made Christmas cookies. (You can't buy any that time of year so I *had* to bake them myself.) I invited all the ladies from the ceramic shop. Needless to say, that ceramic nativity set meant so much to Robert and me. From that time on, we kept it out all year long just to remind us of God's grace and mercy and the wonder of Phyllis and Jim coming to the Lord through Linda's prayers.

Phyllis and I traveled hours together going to towns in Montana or Wyoming where I had speaking engagements. Those hours were full of getting acquainted since our backgrounds were so different. We talked about our boys. We talked about our husbands. We talked about clothes, shoes, decorating—everything. There were hours of talking about spiritual things. And she would ask questions and questions and questions! Questions like "Why do you people do this? Why do you people do that?"

I remember one time when we were down in the middle of Wyoming. It was nearly midnight. (I usually go to bed at 10 p.m. I am a morning person and Phyllis is a night person.) She said, "What happens to your soul when you die? What do you people think about that?"

I grabbed my pillow and just threw it at her. I told her we would talk about it in the morning. I couldn't answer any more questions that night. I was half-kidding and half serious!

Those of us who were raised in the church say things out of habit. Sometimes our beliefs are just handed down with the rest of our earthly possessions when we leave the home of our parents. Now I had to examine what I believed. We spent a lot of time together and we were both growing in our faith. Our friendship continued to grow as well.

We organized a church camping trip to my parents' ranch. We went two days early to help with the setting up. The retreat was for the Emmanuel Fellowship (my parents' church) and ours. We had over forty people there. Some brought their campers, others slept in tents and in cabins. We had special music, a special speaker and even a pig roast. What a blessing that was! We realized how well we could work together!

"With me speaking and her singing, we could make a team," I often said. She wrote some songs and poetry that touched my soul. We often met at the church during the week to share and to pray. I learned so many things! I taught her what I knew as well.

Like the fake fingernails. "How did you get your fingernails so long?" I had asked my friend Sharon. My fingernails always show the effects of typing, wallpapering and other sundry household duties. When dressing up for a special occasion I often wished gloves were back in style.

"It's a secret," Sharon answered. But then in a display of true friendship, she went on. "I get them at Target for $2.97. You just glue them on."

Well, I have never been one to deny vanity. We were making plans for an overnight trip to the city. Fingernails for Lois were on our list. It was like slipping back into high school days!

We sat on the bed in our hotel room. All the necessary equipment spread around us to launch my fingers on their beauty trip. Sharon was a seasoned pro. Soon I was practicing dialing the phone and fastening buttons with my fake finery. Oh, how feminine I felt! Pink frosted nail polish. Clear lacquer top coat.

Now I'm a pro also. The great thing I learned is that after a few weeks with the plastic cover job, my own nails grow. Then I take the fake ones off and I have *real* long nails of my own. Sounds terrific, don't it? Femininity at the low, low price of $2.97.

However, to all good deals there are a few drawbacks. In this case, it is the glue. I imagine the reason nail salons charge more is because they spend a bit more on the fastening factor. But I can put up with a few drawbacks, like occasionally, one of my glamorous nails flies off.

A few weeks ago, we were just beginning our main course at a Christian Women's Club dinner. I picked up my fork and it slid out of my hand. It caught my ring finger—my nail to be exact.

Karen was sitting across from me. She flinched and said, "What was that?"

The lady sitting next to her said, "I don't know. Something just flew by my face!"

Now the cheap-nail-owner dilemma: Do I say, "Oh, that was my fingernail?" Or do I just keep my now stark-white, stubby ring finger curled in hiding during dinner?

I 'fessed up, retrieved the bright pink nail, and quickly took my handy-dandy repair glue bottle from my purse. Everyone at the table was very interested in the procedure! My husband swears if I ever get lost, he will just follow my trail of fingernails until I'm found.

6

Her Pew, My Pew

Lois: One fall day I walked into our church as usual. Naturally we were going to the same church. She had "her" pew and I had "my" pew. We were excited about our various ministries for our Lord. This day, as I walked upstairs, I glanced to the side and saw Phyllis in a Sunday school room praying with Kathy. A thought ran through my mind: *It's funny Kathy didn't call me to pray with her. . . .*

I went upstairs and thought about the thought a time or two. That week I thought about the thought a few more times. I was going to call Phyllis to see if she wanted to go to lunch but then I decided not to.

All of a sudden there was this little "thing" inside my brain.

Phyllis: I continued traveling with Lois when she spoke for Christian Women's Club. She encouraged me to tell my story. But I assured her I was just along for the ride. She was talking to the person who hated being up front. Too much was expected of you, and I'd already been that route!

About two or three years after I started this "church stuff," a couple ladies came to Colstrip from Stonecroft Ministries to start a Christian Women's Club. They encouraged me to attend a speaking workshop. Again I assured them this was not my cup of tea.

"Oh, just put it down on paper. It's always good to have that, you know," they told me.

So I began speaking for Christian Women's Club. When people found out I was from Colstrip, they would assume I was Lois, the funny lady with all those ducks. I suppose it was an easy enough mistake to make, but I didn't like it. Especially when they seemed disappointed to find out I wasn't her!

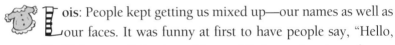 **Lois:** People kept getting us mixed up—our names as well as our faces. It was funny at first to have people say, "Hello, Phyllis" to me all the time. After a while it wasn't quite so funny. I discovered how special my own name was to me. And my place in our church (my church reputation?) was special to me too. I was not perfect. I said often, "God is still working on me." I just didn't realize how comfortably that church-lady title fit—and how much I enjoyed wearing it.

I was visiting with my friend Nan on the phone. She said that she called Phyllis and Phyllis really had helped her. "Phyllis had just the right words to say, knew the right verses and she prayed like no one else had prayed for me before."

I thought of how many times I had prayed with Nan. I had thought that my prayers were pretty good. They surely were as good as Phyllis' prayers . . . weren't they? I wondered why Nan had called Phyllis and not me. My imagination ran wild. I found myself resenting my new friend.

Phyllis: By this time, I was very involved in the church. I sang in the choir, went to Bible studies, even started leading some of them. I wanted to serve. If Jesus loved me enough to change me and change my life, I wanted Him to *have* my life.

When I was asked to head up Vacation Bible School, I was so excited! Until I was told what Lois had done in VBS and how exciting she had made it. She had brought in live ponies for VBS. I was excited about leading a Bible study until I was told how many people came to the Lord when Lois led a recent study.

I guessed maybe I just wouldn't do some things. It seemed wherever I went, Lois had already been there, done that—and done it better than anyone ever had or ever would. I felt like I was walking in Lois' shadow. My friend had just become someone else to measure up to.

Lois: I found many, many times when I walked into church and sat down in my pew that I would turn around to see who Phyllis was talking to. Then I wouldn't want to be friends with whoever it was either. I would turn back toward the front of the church. It felt like I was being replaced, pushed out. It became easier and easier to drop into my own dark, self-inflicted pool of self-pity. I would cry all the way home from church. Things just weren't the same. Church just wasn't the same. I became adept at making it "into" and "out of" my pew without having to speak to Phyllis.

Phyllis: In the next six or eight years, I was a Sunday school teacher for three years, on the worship team for four years and a Sunday school superintendent for four years. I went to every potluck, attended every retreat and attended church every time the doors were open. But in spite of all this, I didn't belong.

I would go in and sit down and feel like I was invisible. The thoughts would go through my mind, *No one cares if you are here or not. They don't need you—they got along just fine before you came. You could be gone six months before they even missed you! You weren't here when they poured the basement—and you'll never catch up!*

The day came when I sat there and thought, *I don't even want to be here!*

I felt out of place and didn't fit in. When they told stories of the "good old days," I only felt more separated from these friends. How could I have these thoughts of loneliness and isolation and yet be so involved? How could I sit on the back row, right-hand side, and not feel like I belonged there? The Sundays I used to love I now dreaded.

And then I overheard someone say she didn't like going to the Wednesday night prayer times because all we did was "pray for Phyllis' boys"—I didn't like church much at all anymore.

Lois: One of the thoughts that was running through my head was that I was getting too old. I didn't want to be one of those "do it my way" ladies. I had heard plenty of sermons about them—the ones that said, "We've always done it this way. . . ." I was determined not to be a fifth wheel. I felt like an extinct dinosaur. *You are out of sync,* I said to myself. (I was doing a lot of talking to myself, replacing the talks I used to have with my friend!) *Church is changing.*

Even worship was different. Now we sang chorus after chorus with an overhead projector beaming the words on a big screen. I thought back, with nostalgic fondness, of the hymnals.

The Colstrip Alliance Church started with a group of us having a Bible study. Later we began Sunday services. We had no hymnals so we mimeographed off some song sheets. We added a blue cover and stapled the sheets together, making little song booklets. During our second year of meeting together, we received a phone call: "The Hardin church had a fire. Their insurance company replaced their smoke-damaged hymnals with new ones. Would you folks like to have the old ones?"

We were elated. Even after scrubbing and scrubbing the covers and trying every home remedy recommended, there was still a tinge of the smoke odor. But we were thrilled with our hymnals. We just took it for granted that we would have a slight smoky smell on our hands after each church service! We laughed about it and praised God for supplying our need.

A few years later we came into church one Sunday to find beautiful burgundy "official" Christian and Missionary Alliance hymnals in the pew racks! They were even engraved with gold letters: "Colstrip Alliance Church." My, how the tears flowed as we held those hymnals in our hands, singing with joy and thankfulness over the anonymous gift. Such a blessing! We felt like a real "grown-up" church.

Now those "blessings" were packed away in a box somewhere.

And the pulpit was gone too. I remember when Randy and Julie Strobel came to the Lord. They had sent their little girls to Daily Vacation Bible School at our church when we were still meeting in a remodeled mobile home by the power plants. A few months after that VBS, Julie began having frightening nightmares. In desperation she decided to call a minister for help. The only one she could think of was the one in "that trailer church the girls had gone to."

Our pastor, Richard Applegate, led her and Randy to the Lord. Within a month, the Strobels' friends Wayne and LaRae Koski came to the Lord. How excited we were! Two families coming to the Lord in one month! Randy was a talented woodworker. When he saw the rickety old table that Pastor Applegate was using as a pulpit, he said, "I can make one. I would love to give it as a gift to my Lord and Savior!" In a few months, the most beautiful, exquisitely made, light oak pulpit was sitting in front of our church. Oh, how thrilled we were. We dedicated it to our Lord, thanking Him for bringing these families into our small congregation.

Now that pulpit was sitting in the back of the church. A black metal music stand was the pulpit of choice now.

A familiar place was no longer familiar. Tradition can be a place of comfort. I had loved the comfort of the place. Now I was seeing a world of change. *What you did was good at one time and you made a big splash, but now you might as well just put yourself on the shelf where you belong,* I told myself. *A younger generation is coming up. God wants to reach them and He is using different ways to reach them.*

I knew and liked the old hymns, but people liked choruses now. I should just be quiet about it.

There were consuming thoughts of the broken friendship. I went before the Lord over and over. *I should call Phyllis,* I would think. *God would want us to straighten this out.* I really missed talking to her, but then I'd say to myself, *There's no use calling because she's probably busy praying with somebody!*

We had the same Lord, we were in the same church, but another difference reared its head. We had some doctrinal differences. There were some things we believed differently and they were coming up in the face of our friendship.

Phyllis: One of the first things I had done in my new life was buy a Bible. I had seen everyone carrying Bibles to church, so I had bought one too. Do you know how much those things can cost?! They can cost $40, $60, $100! I wasn't going to pay that much for a Bible!

So I went to the nearest K-Mart and found one for $9.98. I didn't know how long this good feeling was going to last. (Ceramics only lasted a year.) So I had my $9.98 Bible, and I had Jesus. I met other Christians and we talked and shared what we had learned from the Scriptures.

One of these friends was Nona. She had lived a life similar to mine, and she had met the same Savior. However, she talked more about the Holy Spirit than I did. Nona and I had many heated discussions over the years, but became good friends in spite of our differences. She attended the Foursquare church.

I wanted all God had to offer. If there was more to understand, I wanted to learn what it was about.

Lois: So there I was with my burgundy $52.40 Bible (with a cover). And her with her $9.98 Bible. The interpretation of what we read was different. That was pulling apart our friendship even further. I believed one doctrine. She was beginning to believe another. It was the age-old evangelical-pentecostal debate.

Phyllis: This went on almost four years—the separation process. We didn't travel together anymore. Someone else went with Lois now. We never seemed to "have time" for our coffee times at the Coal Bowl. If Lois and I saw each other we just smiled and spoke: "Hi, how are you?"

"Fine, how are you doing?"

Then we would "happen" to see someone else we "just had to talk to."

On Sunday mornings we went through the same routine—and then quickly found a seat on opposite sides of the room. (She had third row, second pew, left side—I had fifth row, first pew, right side.)

 ois: "Good morning! How are you, Phyllis?"

 hyllis: "Fine, Lois. How are you?"

 ois: "Fine," I'd answer. Then I would run for my pew as she quickly retreated to her pew.

We were both fine, in the same church, attending services and we were both fine.

7

Cancer in Our Midst

Phyllis: Then Lois had to go and get cancer. I thought, *I really feel bad about this. I know we aren't close anymore, but I don't want her to die, for Pete's sake! But I don't know what to do! What if she dies? Then I'll have to live with that guilt!*

Lois: When you discover you have cancer, it does not take long to get real serious with God. Naturally I thought I was going to die.

Now I have cancer, I said to myself. *I am going to get called right up to heaven and the first thing God is going to say to me is, "What did you do about Phyllis?"*

Please don't get the idea that this matter of a broken friendship did not bring us conviction and guilt before this period of time. We had even met together a few times. We would ask each other's forgiveness for "any bad attitudes or wrong motives." Things would seem better for a little while and then we would retreat right back into our desperate, lonely, misguided islands of despair.

We both had spent hours crying and praying about this mess. We just couldn't seem to climb over the walls to victory.

As I had surgery and began cancer treatment, we were both pray-ing about our friendship more fervently. (A life-threatening illness can tend to sharpen the teeth of our praying!)

Now we were serious.

We knew the broken friendship was wrong. I asked God how I could be a friend with Phyllis: "I don't even like her much anymore, God. She believes differently than I do. We just don't have anything in common. We don't even have the same friends." I remembered a printed note that is in *The Friendships of Women* by Dee Brestin (Victor Books). It said: "Dear Ramona, How are you? I am fine. Would you like to be best friends? I like you better than Holly. I don't like Holly anymore. Let's not like Holly together. Your Best Friend, Kate."

Often when women's friendships break, we take others with us. I had committed that sin as well. The Lord kept saying, "Pray for your enemy." I had an enemy in my church and she used to be my best friend. I prayed for Phyllis.

I asked Robert one time why he thought I wasn't able to get vic-tory over this relationship thing. I told him I was praying for her. He said, "You were praying that the Lord would make her more like you or pick her up and move her right out of town!" I think he was only half-kidding.

I was feeling like a dirty rag. I saw my sin. I wrote about that night when victory finally came in my book *Breast Cancer and Me*:

> In the middle of the night. In a motel room the night before surgery. The regular breathing of Robert, sound asleep, is even depressing. Alone. No, I am not alone. Cancer, my unin-vited guest, is having a picnic in my body. . . .
>
> *Oh Lord God, please come to my rescue. I'm in trouble. My en-emies are playing with my mind. Oh Lord, I don't think I'm qualified for this job You have for me. . . . I'm not worthy. . . . There is sin in my life, Lord. You know it, and I know it. There are things that I don't have victory over.*

The still, small voice of the Holy Spirit said, "No, Lois, you are not worthy."

My mind turned into a courtroom. I was both judge and jury. Death could be on the agenda. There was a pile of incriminating evidence on the table between me and my lawyer, my advocate.

The evidence was sin. Unconfessed. Cords of bondage in certain areas. Pleasure of sin enjoyed for a moment. The sin-stack got higher and higher.

[My relationship with my Christian sister, Phyllis, came to mind: my attitudes, my hatefulness . . . my envy . . . my pride . . . selfishness . . . my critical spirit . . . jealousy . . . The list went on and on.]

I looked at myself standing before God. I am a Christian. I love the Lord. I know that when I asked Him to come into my life, years ago, He forgave me my sins.

I knew God's promises:

- "That if thou shalt confess with thy mouth the Lord Jesus, and shalt believe in thine heart that God hath raised him from the dead, thou shalt be saved." (Romans 10:9, KJV)

- "For I will forgive their wickedness and will remember their sins no more." (Hebrews 8:12)

- "As far as the east is from the west, so far has he removed our transgressions from us." (Psalm 103:12)

I knew beyond a shadow of doubt that if I should die, I would go immediately into the presence of the Lord. That's exactly what was causing me to toss and turn. I didn't want to go into His holy presence with unconfessed sin on my hands [and broken relationships scattered behind me].

I stood in the courtroom of my mind, guilty. Guilty of hanging on to some unforgiveness. Guilty of lying. Not a big lie. Just a little "white" lie, just a little stretching of the truth. But in this courtroom, facts are facts and a lie is a lie. I went through the sin-stack on the table. Pride. Lust. Envy. Anger. Fluffy little invisible-to-others things in daintily wrapped containers. Covered with pretty, flowered paper and wrapped with lace . . . until now.

I got out of bed and on my knees.

Oh God, have mercy on me, I prayed through my tears. *I can't deal with cancer in my body until I have dealt with the cancer in my soul. I need Your forgiveness. I need Your cleansing. I've been hanging on to things that aren't pure. Some of these things have wrapped cords of bondage around my soul. Oh Lord God, my heavenly Father, I need You to cleanse me. I need Your mercy.*

And for a long time, in the dark of the night, on my knees in the glaring light of my soul's courtroom, I put the sin-stack under the blood of Jesus Christ. One by one I laid them before my lawyer. My advocate.

And it took a long time. A precious long time. A cleansing long time. The light of dawn was breaking through the motel room curtains as Light was breaking through my soul.

Purifying.

Healing.

Mending.

Forgiving. Filling with mercy.

The sun was up. Night had slunk away. *OK, Cancer, let me see your face. I'm ready. I have already experienced victory because of Christ. And this is just the beginning.* (pages 40-43)

My feelings concerning my friend, Phyllis, were healed. Love had returned.

The Lord showed me when I prayed that I wanted to control her. I wanted to make her like me. I wanted her to go to the same church, wear the same dresses, believe the same verses, believe the same doctrine and be a carbon copy of me. It was very important to me that she believe as I did. That wasn't a pretty picture.

God forgave me. He cleansed my sin. She didn't belong to me; she belonged to Him. There is a big difference in caring for someone and trying to control someone. God forgave me for the thoughts, attitudes and feelings I had had. First John 1:9 says, "If we confess our sins, he is faithful and just and will forgive us our sins and purify us from all unrighteousness."

✳ ✳ ✳

Fix My Eyes

Help me fix my eyes on You
And listen to Your call
For when I take my eyes off You
That's when I trip and fall.

Phyllis Rowe © 2000

8

Retreat Behind the Woodshed

 Phyllis: I said before that God wasn't pleased with my attitude. Now here I am in church having a "new attitude."

I hadn't known you could have "an attitude" if you were a Christian! I asked God to forgive me for—what was it? Resentment? Criticism? Jealousy? I just wanted these things to go away! I didn't want to be phony. I didn't want to pretend nothing was wrong. But I knew the thoughts and feelings I was having were not pleasing to my Lord. I just couldn't get my mind to shut up and do what my heart was telling it. Or maybe my mind was just echoing what was hidden deep in the closet of my heart. I wanted to be real, but the "real" was more than I could deal with.

When someone would comment on something good Lois had done I would snarl on the inside.

I just kept praying, "Lord, show me . . . Lord, help me . . . Lord, cleanse me . . ." and it seemed to get better for a while. Then it would happen all over again. Sometimes I wished I'd never started this "Christian stuff."

At least before I started going to church and reading my Bible, I never knew these feelings were wrong. I always said, "That's just the way I am." Now the Holy Spirit was revealing things I'd rather not know about!

By this time I would gladly have given up my jeans! Jesus was cleansing all right, but it seemed that the more He cleaned, the more He found! My house definitely wasn't clean yet!

Then there was a retreat in Bozeman, Montana. Several ladies were going. I decided I would go too. I had heard Lois was going but I figured it would be safe because there would be 400 ladies there. Surely we could avoid each other in that much space and crowd. The trip up was great. The ladies in my car laughed and shared their "goodie bags." It was going to be a good weekend.

As we gathered in the large room that evening to listen to the speaker, my heart was waiting expectantly to see what God would reveal to us. I just knew it was going to be good! As the speaker began, the door opened and someone came in late. It was Lois. People started whispering, "It's Lois! She's alive! I heard she had cancer! She looks great!"

I thought, *Well, well, she's arrived . . . making a grand entrance.*

Later Jim called as he usually did to see if I had made it and how things were going.

I said, "The evening was OK. The speaker was sort of interesting. Her name is Charlotte Stemple. I think she's the head of something. She talked about forgiveness and stuff."

We went back to our rooms, ate our munchies and got into the deep, late-night talking that makes for a good retreat. Somehow when the lights are out and you are just lying there, you begin to share. I listened and sometimes commented as first Linda, then Elaina and then Nan shared some of their struggles and their victories.

I had some good advice for them.

And then Nan (bless her heart) asked what the Lord was showing me.

I said, "Well, I've got this thing with Lois." They sort of laughed. (They already knew.) I don't know why we think we are hiding our sins so well. Sometimes—most times—others see them before we do. I told them how I struggled and how ashamed I was of my thoughts, and most of all, my heart. I said I didn't know how to get past it or what to do about it. By this time we were all crying. I told them, "I don't even know what to pray anymore."

Nan prayed for God to show me what it was.

All of a sudden the words came to me, "Who are you to judge another?" (James 4:12, NKJV).

That's what I was doing! I was judging her. No one could be that perfect, walk around with a smile all the time—that was just dumb. No one could possibly measure up to her, I reasoned, so she couldn't be real.

At 4 o'clock in the morning I rolled out of bed in that Bozeman, Montana motel room and prayed for the Lord to forgive me.

"Lord, You are right. I have been judging her. Who am I to judge another? Please forgive me, Lord, and cleanse me of this. I am so sorry. In Jesus' name, amen."

The next morning before breakfast, I hurried down to the room of the ladies from the Baptist church to have them go with us. I pounded on their door and when it opened, there stood Lois! She'd gone to visit them too!

We both caught our breath. She invited me in. I walked in and we sat down. We visited with our friends. Something was different. The wall that had been between us seemed to be gone.

I ran back to my room. I told them what had happened, "Lois was there and when I looked into her eyes I knew whatever had been between us was gone." We laughed and cried, grateful to see what God had done.

Nan and Linda went down to breakfast. Elaina and I redid our make-up. The speaker had started when we arrived so we were late. In the room of 400 ladies we found the last two seats. I quickly sat down, turned my coffee cup right side up—and brushed elbows with Lois.

We said "Hello" and got very quiet.

I believe we sensed God was doing something. We talked small talk. Then Lois put her spoon down carefully and said, "Phyllis, would you like to stay and ride back to Colstrip with me? I am going to stop at the ranch on the way home and spend the night. Would you like to go?"

There was a bit of fear in taking a four-hour ride with someone I had hardly talked to in months. I told her I would think about it.

Someone would need to take our new car home. We had just gotten it. It still had the sticker in the window. I went back to the room and told my "late-night" friends about the conversation between Lois and myself. We cried again. Linda quickly volunteered to drive our new car. (Bless her heart.)

I went with Lois, and we spent the night at the ranch with her folks. The next day on the four-hour trip home we talked . . . carefully. We were very cautious in the subjects we approached. We knew we needed to "get below the surface," but just how deep could we go before it got "touchy"? We knew God was restoring us, and we wanted to be careful. The healing had begun.

Lois: Some time later I was asked to speak at the Northern Cheyenne prayer lodge. I asked Phyllis to come and share together with me. Phyllis had been in to talk to the pastor. She told him about the speaking date. He said, "That's nice."

"No," she said. "That is a miracle."

And it was a miracle.

We thank our Lord and Savior, Jesus Christ, for working that miracle, for restoring our broken hearts and broken friendship. We thank Him for revealing and forgiving our sins of judging, envy, criticizing and pride. We thank Him for the miracle of restoration. We started over . . .

. . . building bridges instead of walls.

We throw away a dress when it has a stain.
    We throw away nylons when they get a run,
        and a cup when the handle breaks.

But we cannot throw away a broken friendship.
    It is too valuable.

> *"For we are his workmanship, created in Christ Jesus
>   unto good works, which God hath before ordained
>   that we should walk in them." (Ephesians 2:10, KJV)*

9

It Ain't Easy, Lord... Sandpaper Relationships

ois: A few years ago I was asked to cook at church camp. I was so excited about being asked to cook. That doesn't happen very often to someone who once made gravy out of plaster of paris!

I ironed aprons for weeks. I told everyone what I was going to do. The first year I made Kool-Aid, filled the salt and pepper shakers and cooked peas. I was so excited about how good I had done that I wrote a whole paragraph about it in our Christmas letter. The next year I was asked back. I parked in "my" spot and did cake mixes and other vegetables. That was grand.

"I have done so well in years past," I told Robert the next spring, "that soon I will probably be asked to be head cook."

They called in June. The head cook, Beulah, said that there was a cook who had canceled and could I bring someone else with me?

I thought of a lady who had five kids who all looked healthy and asked her to go with me. It started out fine but by the third day I didn't like this lady much anymore. See, I had these aprons all lying out to match my outfits and she just pushed them around. I also needed my sleep and she slept too noisily in my little trailer. I lay in bed in the middle of the night with my glasses on and thought that the woman was going to have a heart attack.

We went down for breakfast on Wednesday morning and planned our day. I liked this part of the day because we could sit and drink coffee. The head cook said it would be meat loaf for lunch and tuna fish with white sauce over biscuits for supper. My used-to-be friend volunteered for meat loaf. So I volunteered for biscuits.

The head cook said this was the way we would do it: mix the dry ingredients before breakfast. Later I could add water. She said to double the recipe.

So I had the recipe and was reading everything carefully . . . with one eye. With the other eye I was watching my-used-to-be-friend. She went to work on the meatloaf without the recipe. It was awful watching her! She just stuck her hand in the salt sack and took some salt out! I don't care if everyone does say she is such a good cook—she should use the recipe. I knew everyone would say, "Remember that year Lois brought the friend who wrecked the meat loaf?" My reputation would be ruined.

At lunch everyone ranted and raved over how good the meat loaf was. I thought it was salty. But I told her it was nice and went back to my perfect biscuits. I had about a hundred of them cut out nicely on the pan. Then a lightbulb went off in my head. I realized what I had done! I had put baking soda in them instead of baking powder!

Beulah (she's still the head cook) said we would put a couple in the oven and see what happened. When they came out of the oven, they looked like and tasted like pregnant Alka-Seltzer. She said that honey and jelly were out, but if we smothered them in tuna fish gravy we could make it through the meal!

The camp evangelist came in the last day to talk to Beulah, telling her that with all his traveling he had problems with his stomach. Since Thursday he hadn't had to take a single Tums!

(I also need to tell you how these Christians really act. That year under our Christmas tree there was a beautiful box all wrapped in gold foil with a gorgeous red and gold ribbon. When I opened it, it had two of those little biscuits in it, with a note "Love from the camp cooks!")

After I had made those biscuits I went running out and up the hill to the nearest pine tree. I cried and I cried. I wasn't crying about the biscuits. I was crying because the Lord had shown me my critical spirit. I was so critical of my friend that I couldn't even pay attention to what I was doing. I thought of how critical I'd become of my husband, the pastor's wife and ladies in Christian Women's Club. The list went on and on.

I prayed and confessed that critical spirit to the Lord. Because I know He forgives, I could get up and go back to the kitchen and do the hard part—I had to ask forgiveness from my friend from Colstrip. God taught me a valuable lesson that day. He had been trying to get my attention. I just wasn't listening. It took the biscuits to teach me the pain, the sin and the destruction a critical spirit can cause. Sometimes it is a critical spirit that destroys a friendship.

Phyllis: Lois and I had never actually had "words" or a knockdown, drag-out fight. I guess she was too nice to fight and I didn't know how to fight nice! However, there have been times when the words were spoken by other Christians and they pierced like an arrow.

- "You aren't leadership material as far as I am concerned."

- "I've never felt you should be involved in that ministry. That ministry requires someone with much fruit evident in her life."

- "You are just like a bulldozer—determined to get your way!"

- "I have never respected you in that position in the church."

- "You always start things and don't finish them."

God will sometimes use people we don't like
To say things we don't like to hear
To accomplish the work He wants to do in us.

Does that mean we can freely speak our opinions to each other regardless of outcome? No. It simply means when those hurtful words are spoken to us, or about us, God will work it out for good when we seek Him in the midst of it.

- What do you do about the times when the hurtful, critical, words are spoken?

- What do you do when the angry words come out for everyone to hear and talk about?

- What do you do when the situation is real and painful?

Those spoken words can run through our minds over and over like a broken record. When we entertain them and let them take hold, we become hindered in our effectiveness for the Lord.

When we are the ones speaking those words, we become a very effective tool of the enemy, if we aren't speaking from a heart of love and genuine concern for the person.

Maybe you are dealing with a situation where those words came out and everyone is talking about it (in a very Christian way, of course). Remember, it's the heart attitude that the Lord looks at. He knows every word spoken and unspoken.

I want to be genuine on the inside. I want my heart to be pure. I don't want to say the "right things" but on the inside be the same ugly person. Do you ever struggle with that, or is it just me?

One time I was in disagreement with some things happening in the church and with some of the people. I was sure they were handling a situation wrong. As the days went on, I found my prayer times were becoming empty and flat. I cried out to the Lord, but He seemed silent. I didn't sense that quiet Presence as I waited. Finally, standing with my hands in dishwater, praying, I asked, "Lord, what is wrong between us?"

The Lord spoke very clearly to me. He said, "You are criticizing My children."

Have you ever had anyone criticize your children? Believe me, I knew what that felt like! I had spent years listening to first one, and then another tell me all the things my sons were doing wrong. I knew what my boys were like and I loved them anyway. I didn't need someone else telling me about it. I knew my children better than anyone else. Even though I may not have admitted some of their wrongs, it didn't mean I was blind to them. Why would I think God liked it any better when I criticized His kids?

We are God's children and He knows us. We as earthly parents can get upset when our children are criticized. Why do we not consider the idea that God would be unhappy with our criticisms and judgments of each other? He knows the whole situation. We only see a part of it.

From the time Jaree was two years old she has gone to church with Jim and me. When she was about five years old, she started reaching into my purse when the offering basket went by, taking some money out to put in it. I thought she was being cute, and besides, it was good for her to get used to giving to the Lord.

This went on for some time. She always leaned over and whispered, "Gramma, give me some money to put in!" One Sunday when I was preoccupied, she got in my purse and grabbed frantically at a $5 bill. Now this was the week before payday and this was part of the "milk and bread" money.

"Honey," I said, "that's too much. Here, put this dollar in."

I'll never forget the look on her face. Realizing something was very wrong, I took her out to the foyer and asked what it was.

"Gramma," she said softly with tears in her eyes, "we never put any money in the plate for Jesus."

Shocked, and with a lump in my throat, I reassured her that we did.

"No, Gramma! I always watch, and you never put any in! And today you said I was putting in too much!" By this time we were both crying.

I don't know what message was being given in the sanctuary, but I was getting mine in the foyer!

"Honey, is that why you are always getting money from my purse for the offering basket?"

"Yes," she replied. "Everyone else gives money to Jesus."

As I held her tight I thought of all those Sundays when I thought she was just being "cute." And I thought of how she must have felt when I told her it was "too much."

And I cried.

Then I explained that Grampa always put our money in for Jesus, and he knew just how much to give.

"Are you sure?" she sniffed.

"Positive," I replied.

No wonder God calls us His "children." Sometimes we only see a part of a situation and can misinterpret what we do see. Only the Lord knows the hearts of His children and can judge our motives and actions.

ois: Sometimes those hurts come from without. Not only in church situations, but in family, work and even traffic situations. There are public hurts as Phyllis mentioned, but there are also other kinds of hurts that only we know about. There can be offenses that are intentional and those that are unintentional.

I remember whining to the Lord that I was the only one in the church who did anything. I cleaned up after each potluck. I was always calling the pastor saying that so-and-so needs a bouquet and a visit. "It seems like I am the only one who cleans the children's church room and does Vacation Bible School stuff," I told the Lord one day. I asked Him to send someone else. Then Phyllis showed up to help—and I was angry because she was on my turf!

Silly? Of course! But at the time it didn't seem silly.

The Lord answered my prayer and now I was allowing selfishness and pride and self-pity to take the place of the gratitude for the help I prayed for! She was on "my church turf."

Oh, how hurts that we allow to eat away at us and destroy our servant's hearts often have to do with church turf.

One lady related to us how happy she was to move to a city where there was a church of her denomination. She quickly volunteered to help with Meals On Wheels. The church coordinated the delivery of meals to house-bound senior citizens. On the first assigned day, Maggie pulled her car in front of the Senior Citizen Center. She was a little early but she was anxious to meet some of the other women so she went right in. She felt some awkward looks. Only one woman, definitely an outsider with the "in" group, made an attempt to welcome her. "Did I do something wrong?" Maggie asked her.

"Yes," admitted her new acquaintance. "You parked in our chapter president's spot."

Maggie went on to tell me that the woman was still cool to her at church functions!

Oh, how we want to protect our turf!

We were invited to a retreat two years ago. Phyllis was going to sing and I would be speaking. When we arrived, we noticed a woman who was quite aggravated as she walked away from the registration table. We overheard her say to her friend, "If they can't even spell my name right, you can bet your boots that I will never come back to one of their precious retreats!"

Oh, how we allow our pride to rule our attitudes at times!

Recently, the wife of a pastor told me that in the first year of their ministry, a woman in their church called her aside to tell her, "Are you aware that most of the women in this church hate you?"

By the time this wife found that statement was not true, the damage had already been done. Her self-esteem and confidence had been ripped away.

Oh, the damage of a spiteful tongue!

Another woman came up to us after she attended our seminar. She said that she worked in a music store. "My boss is an atheist," she told us. "He told me he could never believe in the God of some of the Christians who had been customers in his store. If you could only see the fights, arguments and words spoken in anger by people on the music committees in that store over buying a church piano or organ, you would understand why he felt that way!"

Oh, those sandpaper people!

I was telling a friend about meeting a niece of hers at a retreat in North Dakota. "She is a Christian," I related happily. "She says she asked Jesus into her heart six years ago."

My friend's remark was, "You'd think if she was such a fine Christian, she'd try harder to get along with her family!"

Oh, the ones who know us best . . . hurt the most!

Words

Hateful words . . .
Spiteful words . . .
Words that rip and tear
Words that cause us hurt and pain
More than we can bear.

Critical words . . .
Judging words . . .
Spoken from hearts of sin
Words that crush
Words that wound
And wither the soul within.

Words of peace . . .
Words of love . . .
Words that build and mend
Words that lift our heart in song
And bring hope without limit or end.

Only you can make the choice . . .

Are you a vessel God can use?
Which words will you speak?
Which words will you choose?

Phyllis Rowe © 2000

10

"Did You Say, 'In One Accord,' Lord?"

Lois: We tell you about these experiences because we want you to know, not only from us, but in examples of other people, that broken relationships, hurt feelings and angry words are happening all around us. The lack of love and compassion and forgiveness for each other is tearing down our witness in this world. It is time to bring our feelings and broken relationships into the open and learn how to deal with them. It is time to take our church relationships seriously. God tells us to love one an-other—and He was talking to the kids in His family—us!

Phyllis: Lois and I don't go to the same church any-more. It has nothing to do with our friendship. We still have our differences, but we have learned to respect each other's beliefs. God is using Lois right where she is, and He is using me right where I am.

We respect each other, love each other and trust God for both of us.

Through circumstances and timing, Jim and I felt we were to leave the church where God had first put us. We have many wonderful memories of our years there. And some are not so wonderful. But we grew, learned and loved and were loved in return. It was very painful to leave.

Have you ever considered why we attend the churches we do? As I thought about this over the months and years, I realized there are several reasons:

- Our family has always attended that church.
- Some of our best friends go there.
- They have a fantastic youth group (or nursery set-up or . . .).
- The building itself is just wonderful.
- We like the pastor.
- It's the closest to our home.

Sometimes we spend more time checking out a new dress shop or a new garage than we spend checking out the church we attend. What about the doctrine of the church? Do you know the basic foundation of belief in that denomination? Do you fully understand it? Are you in agreement with the theology taught in that church? Do you understand the Scriptures the same way?

I know we won't always agree on every single issue. Are you in agreement with the main doctrine of the church and what is being taught and practiced? If you aren't sure you understand, talk to the pastor.

The Bible says wonderful things happened when the new Church was "all in one accord."

Jim and I now attend the church down the street. I'm again the new kid on the block. This time I'm not a baby Christian, and I'm trying to be careful. "Lord, let me learn from my mistakes."

I joined the worship team some time ago. I asked Trish if this was OK with her since she was new to the team as well. I explained to her that my voice range wasn't as wide as hers, and that I didn't read music. There may be some songs that I would just have to sing where I could find the range of the notes in harmony, and would she be willing to work around me? She said that was fine, and she would be happy to work with me. (Colleen and Jeff were the worship leaders and they were happy with both of us.)

At another time, I noticed some decorations on the church walls that needed to be changed. They were looking a little ragged and dusty. I wanted something to do. I talked with the pastor about changing them. He said that was fine as long as I didn't make it "flinky." I went home and thought about it and had to go back to him and ask what he thought "flinky" was. (It means "prissy"!)

I also asked who had done the work before, and would "they" be hurt if I changed some things. It turned out "they" had moved out of town. So there wasn't a problem.

My friend Colleen had done some of the decorations. I asked her if she would be offended if I redid some of them. Being Colleen, she laughed and said, "You know me—that's definitely not my gifting! I just put it there to have something to put there! Do whatever you want!"

We need to ask the Lord to make us more sensitive to each other. How will the other person respond? How can we work together?

Lois: Phyllis and I were laughing about this. I told her she should just stay in a church long enough to redo all the worn-down and worn-out floral arrangements. She could redecorate the bathrooms like she did in our church and the church she is in now. Then she could move to a different church in Colstrip.

Soon every church would be a place of beauty and fixed up like it ought to be. She does beautiful flower arrangements.

That's how a church works: we all make up the body. We all have our individual personalities and special gifts. God wants us to use them all together. One flower shouldn't resent the other—they should all work together to create a beautiful arrangement.

> *"Fulfil ye my joy, that ye be likeminded, having the same love, being of one accord, of one mind. Let nothing be done through strife or vainglory; but in lowliness of mind let each esteem other better than themselves." (Philippians 2:2-3, KJV)*

11

A Pattern for Restoration

 Phyllis: Is the Lord showing you something you need to let Him work on? It may not be a friendship, as it was for us, that God has brought to your mind as you read this. Whatever it is, let God do His work in you.

The only way we can be content in serving the Lord is to be yielded to His Spirit at work within us. My new prayer is (grammar not withstanding!), "Lord, whatever this lesson is, let me learn it quick, and let me get it right the first time."

Search My Heart

Ask God to search your heart. Sometimes we can be so busy recounting what was said or done to us that we don't stop to look at our own words or actions. If we do look at them, the first thing we want to do is excuse our part or rationalize it.

Don't look at others. This is just between you and God. Admit that your attitude, your heart and your words aren't right. Psalm 139:23-24 says, "Search me, O God, and know my heart; test me and know my anxious thoughts. See if there is any offensive way in me, and lead me in the way everlasting."

Some questions we may need to ask ourselves as we allow God to search our hearts are:

- What is my motive for my actions or words in this situation?
- Do I just want to look good to others in this situation?
- Am I worried about what people will think of me?
- Am I afraid of being proven wrong?
- Am I expecting something in return? (If I do this, then I expect you to do that?)

Don't be too quick to answer this. Wait for a moment before the Lord, and ask Him to reveal any hidden motives that may not be glorifying to Him.

> And whatever you do, do it heartily, as to the Lord and not to men, knowing that from the Lord you will receive the reward of the inheritance; for you serve the Lord Christ. (Colossians 3:23-24, NKJV)

We can be so busy looking at somebody else that we don't even consider that there is something we need to look at in our own hearts. Search me, O God.

When He shows you something, don't *argue* with Him. We tend to do one of several things when God searches our heart and reveals something we don't like.

We try to *ignore* Him. "Oh, I don't think that was from the Lord." When we can't ignore Him any longer we try to *deny* it. "Oh Lord, surely you don't mean I act like that!" When we can no longer ignore Him and what He is saying to us and the conviction is so strong we can't deny it any longer, we have one option left: the *"blame game."* I tend to be quick to say, "Lord, the reason I did that was because they . . ." Instead, pray, "Lord, You are right. My actions and words were not pleasing to You. I'm sorry. Please forgive me."

The only way there is going to be a real difference is to be real before God.

Once when I was struggling through a hurtful situation, I prayed and cried to the Lord about it many times, with no relief. As I sat in my rocking chair with my cup of coffee one day, again taking it to Him, I suddenly saw myself as if standing before my Lord.

It was like once again He was asking me about the situation. I began to tell Him word for word what had been said and how hurt I was. As I heard the words I had prayed—"Lord, she said . . ."—I realized how childish and petty they sounded when placed before a holy, righteous, Almighty God.

In my heart I heard Him say, "Which is more important: hanging on to this or letting it go and getting on with the work I have for you to do?"

Immediately, my heart broke as I realized I had grieved my Lord. "Forgive me, Father. I lay it down. What do you want me to do?"

When we realize we stand before a holy God, somehow dealing with our own sin becomes more important than pointing out the sins of another!

> The sacrifices of God are a broken spirit, a broken and a contrite heart—these, O God, You will not despise. (Psalm 51:17, NKJV)

Love One Another

The second thing to do is love one another. That was not a choice or an option given to us. Second John 5 says, "And now, dear lady, I am not writing you a new command but one we have had from the beginning. I ask that we love one another."

How do you love somebody you don't like?

I have prayed, "Lord, I need to love that person and quite frankly, I don't have it in me." But He is Love and if you ask, you will find yourself loving him or her with God's love. When we cannot love the person ourselves, that's when He will help us.

Sometimes when you let God search your heart, the other person looks a little different because you are seeing him or her through God's eyes. Sometimes as God searches my heart and reveals my sin in the situation or my sinful attitude, I find my focus changing.

Some people are Sandpaper People—they rub us the wrong way. I have found that when God puts me with Sandpaper People, it is usually because He wants to reveal something in me He wants to cleanse. These people tend to "get under my skin" and bring out something *ugly* that I thought I was keeping well hidden (or perhaps was hidden even from me)!

The Lord has been working on me in this area (again). I have cried before Him that I am not a "sweet, loving" person. (I have never been accused of being "sweet"!) He knows that.

Just this week, as I approached the Father about this, I felt He explained something to me. Even though there was love in our home as kids, it wasn't shown in demonstrative ways. The first time I remember someone saying he loved me, it was a boy in my teenage years. (He was a nice boy.) Mom loved us kids but had so many problems and worries that they consumed her thoughts and time. The first time I remembered receiving a hug from Mom was after I was married and living in Montana.

Living in an abusive marriage for sixteen years didn't help with the understanding of love. I don't blame Fred, my ex-husband. He had his own hurts and past to deal with. But I have decided that for the most part, demonstrative loving doesn't come easy for me, and maybe it doesn't for you either. When I do love someone, I sometimes have a hard time showing it. The Lord is working on that area of my life as well.

Sometimes I wonder—will we ever be able to love as the Father loves us?

I want to "go back to my first love." In the busyness of serving, I can forget Who I'm serving. When I take the time to look back at all the wonderful things God has done for me, I'm ashamed of my selfishness. He has loved me with an unconditional love, in spite of all my "attitudes."

> But God demonstrates His own love toward us, in that while we were still sinners, Christ died for us. (Romans 5:8, NKJV)

Whether we don't love as we should, or simply can't show it as we'd like, God commands us to love. We don't have a choice. And since God so demonstrated His love for us, we ought to love one another.

Discern . . . Truth or Lie

We need to be able to discern. Remember all those thoughts going through our heads that Lois and I talked about? Second Corinthians 10:4-5 states—

> For the weapons of our warfare are not carnal but mighty in God for pulling down strongholds, casting down arguments and every high thing that exalts itself against the knowledge of God, bringing every thought into captivity to the obedience of Christ. (NKJV)

Why do we just let our thoughts run rampant? Why do we just assume that every thought going through our minds is just us or from the Lord?

Take those thoughts captive. How do you do that? How do you stop them?

One day, I just said, "Lord, I don't want to think like this, and I don't think these thoughts are from You either. What do I do?" His Word says to take that thought captive. I began to say to those thoughts, "No, in the name of the Lord Jesus, I will not entertain that thought. That is not truth. That is not what I really want to think or say."

When that thought comes out of your mouth, in angry or critical words, you've just become a tool in the hands of the enemy. Dwell on the good things in that person. Philippians 4:8-9 tells us:

> Finally, brethren, whatever things are true, whatever things are noble, whatever things are just, whatever things are pure, whatever things are lovely, whatever things are of good report, if there is any virtue and if there is anything praiseworthy—meditate on these things. The things which you learned and received and heard and saw in me, these do, and the God of peace will be with you. (NKJV)

We don't always have "things of good report" spoken about us, or to us. My first response is to defend myself and deny the things said. The Lord has shown me that even if the words are hurtful, there is usually a grain of truth somewhere, or it wouldn't sting so.

I'm learning to say, "Lord, was there any truth in that? Is there something I need to deal with here?" If there is, *accept the facts, confess it to the Lord* and *let the scrubbing begin!*

If you allow the Lord to search your heart and He finds it innocent, then let it go. Don't dwell on it. Don't allow it to play over and over in your mind. If there's truth—deal with it. Acknowledge it to the Father, ask forgiveness, ask Him to cleanse you of the sin and fill you with His Spirit.

Can God ever receive glory in the hurtful situations? Scripture says,

> Blessed be the God and Father of our Lord Jesus Christ, the Father of mercies and God of all comfort, who comforts us in all our tribulation, that we may be able to comfort those who

are in any trouble, with the comfort with which we ourselves are comforted by God. For as the sufferings of Christ abound in us, so our consolation also abounds through Christ. (2 Corinthians 1:3-5, NKJV)

Sometimes thoughts are just an attack from our enemy. Recently my mind was being bombarded with thoughts that just would not shut up, no matter what I did. I said, "Lord, I've prayed everything I know to pray, confessed everything I know to confess, and nothing is working! I want to go to sleep!"

I felt the Lord said to write the thoughts down on paper. I did that and filled up three pages. Somehow it seemed to help to see them written out. I then prayed about each thought or statement separately. Next, I spoke the truth of Scripture for each of those statements.

Afterward, I didn't know what to do with those ugly words I had written. (I don't know about you, but sometimes my heart and mind are not so lovely.) I certainly didn't want anyone to see them, so I destroyed the pages.

This is not a formula for every occasion, but at this particular time in my life, when the battle was so fierce, this helped. Ask God to help you in the middle of the battle and He will show you the answer to your own situation.

Just as Lois and I shared some of the thoughts that bombarded us, some of our friends have shared thoughts they've had. The enemy knows which buttons to push in each of us.

Do you recognize any of these "buttons"?

- "If they would listen to me, I could tell them a much better way to do that!"

- "It looked/worked/produced much more effectively when I did it!"

- "If I quit, then they'd realize how much I do around here!"

- "Oh, I could never do anything like that. I just don't know how."

- "I'm not going to volunteer—I would just look stupid!"

- "I could never do as good a job as she does."

- "I don't know enough to be a leader."

- "I'm too tired and too old for this. Let someone else do it."

- "Well, I guess I'm just not needed around here anymore."

What are some thoughts that go through your mind that the devil uses to "push your buttons"?

Thoughts	*Truth*
_____	_____
_____	_____
_____	_____
_____	_____
_____	_____
_____	_____
_____	_____
_____	_____
_____	_____

Pray and ask the Lord to help you discern.
Would you find the context of the thought in Scripture?
What is God's truth about the issue?

Confess to the Lord that you have allowed this way of thinking to influence your attitudes and words. Ask His forgiveness. Write the scriptural truth about the situation or person. Pray for the other person—or for the situation.

Take the thoughts captive and ask the Lord to help you discern. Do they line up with what God's Word says is truth about you? Or are they lies and taunts from the enemy, designed to keep you from serving the Lord you love?

> Be anxious for nothing, but in everything by prayer and supplication, with thanksgiving, let your requests be made known to God; and the peace of God, which surpasses all understanding, will guard your hearts and minds through Christ Jesus. (Philippians 4:6-7, NKJV)

Be Willing To . . .

We need to be willing to do whatever we need to do to change the situation. Romans 12:18 says, "If it is possible, as far as it depends on you, live at peace with everyone."

We need to be willing to change—willing to surrender.

1. You need to be willing to surrender your position:

- Who I am
- How long I've been here
- All that I do and have done
- Who I'm not—"I'm not the_____, why should I _____?"

There is no seniority in Jesus. He actually said, "Many who are first will be last, and many who are last will be first" (Matthew 19:30). I never understood that verse exactly, but it seems to me it could fit for the places of seniority we sometimes feel we have achieved. Sometimes we feel we have a reputation or "witness of Christ" to protect. Usually, if we are honest with ourselves, that simply means we want to "look good" to others. Are we to be good "ambassadors for Christ" (2 Corinthians 5:20, NKJV)? Absolutely. But it's for His glory—not ours.

2. We need to be willing to surrender our "self"

- Our ideas and our opinions
- Our likes and dislikes
- What we want and what we need
- Our emotions and our "feelings"

Did you ever wait all week for something on TV you wanted to watch, and just as it came on, someone called and had a "crisis situation"? You got back to the show just in time to watch the credits roll down the screen. How did you handle that?

Or you haven't eaten all day, the meal is on the table—and the telephone rings or someone is at the door with a problem.

Or you are asked to do something on a certain day each week—and it just happens to be on the only day you could have some time alone to read, shop, golf, etc.

How much of our "self" are we willing to sacrifice? Are we willing to give up our own time to help someone else? How willing are we to do without something so someone else can have? (Remember Uncle Burl and the "treats" left in the lunch box?)

One of the worst prayers I ever prayed was, "Lord, please show me my self in everyday situations. I want to be more like You and less like me."

It was amazing how much self showed up. She was looking for the best parking space at the post office. She was listening to make sure she got the credit for things she did. She made sure she got more cherries in her bowl of ice cream than her husband. She even made sure the plumper pillow was on her side of the bed. Her ideas were the best ones offered at church functions, and she felt her opinion should carry as much weight as anyone else's. After all, wasn't she _____ ?

Do I still struggle with that? Yes, sometimes. There's an ample supply of self. I don't pray that prayer anymore. It seems once was enough.

> And let us consider one another in order to stir up love and good works. (Hebrews 10:24, NKJV)

3. Are you willing to surrender as Jesus did?

His position. He left the realms of glory to come and dwell among us. Some of His best friends were fishermen. He ate fish on the seashore. His place wasn't always at the head table.

His reputation. Many people didn't like Jesus or approve of His work. He didn't waste His time worrying about what they thought. He only sought His Father's will. Jesus was not a "people-pleaser." He was not always popular.

He gave *His very life*—how can we hold on to anything of ourselves when Jesus gave up everything for us? He sacrificed His own life blood for us. He gave up His life in dying for us. We can give up our life in living for Him.

Do What?

"Die to self" is what Paul would say
The pastor preached it the other day
It must be important, or so it seems,
And I surely would do it
If I knew what it means!!

Phyllis Rowe © 2000

He says that when we will lay ourselves down He will lift us up. We need to let Him work His way in us.

Let this mind be in you which was also in Christ Jesus, who, being in the form of God, did not consider it robbery to be equal with God, but made Himself of no reputation, taking the form of a bondservant, and coming in the likeness of men. And being found in appearance as a man, He humbled Himself and became obedient to the point of death, even the death of the cross. (Philippians 2:5-8, NKJV)

Forgiveness, like love, is not a choice.

Jesus said to forgive seventy times seven (Matthew 18:22, NKJV). Does forgiving mean that what they did was all right? No. Is forgiveness free license to do it again? No.

Things have been said and done, and the hurts are real. Forgiveness means we aren't willing to let that hurt control our emotions and thinking anymore. As we forgive those who hurt us, it releases the healing power of God into our hearts and minds, and into the relationship with the other person. It was the forgiveness of our sin that first brought us into the kingdom of God. How can we do any less? The Lord Jesus paved the way with His blood.

God showed me that with my ex-husband. I was reading through the book of Matthew. In 6:15 He says, "But if you do not forgive men their trespasses, neither will your Father forgive your trespasses" (NKJV). I remembered all the black eyes and the pain. Most of all, I remembered all those hurtful words. I started to argue with the Lord and then He reminded me of some things I had done in the marriage. I realized my sin was as great as Fred's. I had hurt him too. I just rationalized my sin and weighed it on my "scale" of who did the most wrong. (I told you I was good at doing that.) I knew I needed to resolve this with Fred.

Kelly was still in Elko with Fred and had been dating a girl he had known in high school. They had decided to get married, and we were going down for the wedding. I told Jim I felt the Lord wanted me to talk with Fred, and he said, "OK."

At the wedding reception, I asked Fred to go out in the hallway with me. I told him I needed to talk to him.

As we stepped out I said, "Fred, Jim and I are trying to serve the Lord now, and I want my heart to be right before Him. So I'm asking your forgiveness for my part of the marriage."

The man who used to blacken my eyes got tears in his. "Phyllis, you were forgiven a long time ago. Will you forgive me?"

I gladly forgave him, and as we hugged, Jim walked out into the hallway. There is now a good relationship between my ex-husband and myself. It brought healing to all involved. The boys are now more comfortable with all of us. We can talk to and about each other in peace.

The best news is that a few years later, when we were visiting with Kelly and Tammy, Fred came out to visit and have coffee with all of us. The Lord led us into a conversation that ended with Fred taking Jesus home with him!

Unforgiveness locks God away from the situation. Forgiveness opens the door for God to love.

God is good and He has done His part. We have to learn to let go of self—our opinions, our feelings—and ask for forgiveness, and forgive. In my situation, the Lord showed me that I had to ask forgiveness for my part of the marriage. Forgiving Fred was only part of it. Sometimes we can be so grand and religious and spiritual. We say we forgive, but we still have a wrong heart attitude.

Once when I was speaking on this subject at a meeting, the Holy Spirit prompted me to address the way we forgive. I spoke on the way we can say, "Oh, I forgive you" with such a pious attitude that it grieves the heart of the Father. (And the other person isn't fooled either.)

Afterward, a lady came up to me with tears in her eyes and said softly, "You were speaking just to me. I have lorded it over my family for years, as I grandly 'forgave' them for the 'hurts' they've caused me."

When we truly forgive with the heart of compassion and love that Jesus portrayed, then healing can flow.

Shayla is Kelly and Tammy's little girl. She is four and likes to call her Gramma every chance she gets. One evening the telephone rang and I heard Shayla's little voice, quivering with tears. "Gramma? Do you know what my puppy did? She bited my lip, and it's bweeding."

"Oh, honey, I'm sorry she bit you. Are you OK?"

"No, Gramma, I told you, it's bweeding!"

"Well, honey, can you forgive her?"

"Yes, Gramma," she sighed, "I can forgive her. She's just a wittle puppy."

I'm glad Shayla is learning to forgive when she's "wittle," and not waiting until she's "big" like her Gramma.

A word of caution: If people don't know that you have had unloving, critical thoughts about them . . . don't go and tell them! Don't ask forgiveness or grant forgiveness out loud if they have no idea anything is wrong between you. You will just dump your garbage on them and leave them holding a stinking bag.

A lady approached me one afternoon and said, "I'm so glad you said that. A woman came up to me several months ago, and 'confessed' that she had been very angry with me for a position I had taken in the church. She said she had 'bad-mouthed' me to all her friends. She then asked my forgiveness and walked away while I stood there feeling like someone had just thrown up all over me. It took me a while to let all that go."

If the other person is aware of the problem, then talk. If they don't know, don't tell them. It will suffice to tell it to the Lord as you ask His forgiveness.

We need to be willing to change. God does not expect us to be perfect, but He does expect progress. We should not be the same Christian we were ten years ago—or even yesterday.

I love my daughter-in-law, Tammy. She blesses me every time the telephone rings and I hear her, "Hi, whatcha doin'?"

God has made some wonderful changes in the life of my son Kelly, but sometimes Tammy needs to "vent" to someone, and who better than his mom who loves them both?

She was telling me recently that in a conversation with Kelly he said, "You're praying for me again, aren't you? I could always tell when Mom was praying for me!"

I laughed and said, "Tammy, tell him Mom didn't quit. God just sent reinforcements!"

Levi is their son and they are sending him to a Christian school. So when Mom and Tammy aren't praying, Levi is practicing his Scripture memorization out loud as he goes around the house! (God is very faithful.)

Are you willing to let God change you? Sometimes we sit with folded arms because we don't think we need to change. It's easier to think it's the other person God is talking to. We need to allow God to search our hearts and show us what needs to be changed.

Kevin went through some hard years before he allowed God to make some drastic changes in his life. He has been sober for almost three years and is beginning to realize the joy and freedom that can come in a life surrendered to the Lord Jesus. He is enjoying life—and we are enjoying him.

Jayci is Jaree's little sister. She spends a lot of time at my house and we enjoy her tremendously. One day she wandered into the kitchen while I cooked supper, and said, "Gramma, do you have any pickles?"

"Oh, I think so," I answered.

"Can I have one?" she asked as she opened up the refrigerator door.

"I suppose so." I wiped my hands and proceeded to get a fork to get the pickle.

"Gramma, what kind of pickles are they?"

"I don't know, Jayci," I answered as I quickly stabbed at a slippery one.

"Well," she insisted, "are they kosher dills?"

"I don't know! What difference does it make?"

"Well," she said, as she crunched the first bite of the pickle and left the room, "they could be daffodils."

Sometimes I think we are
trying so hard to be kosher dills . . .
when all along God wants us to be daffodils.

Now the Lord is the Spirit; and where the Spirit of the Lord is,
there is liberty. But we all, with unveiled face, beholding as
in a mirror the glory of the Lord, are being transformed
into the same image from glory to glory, just as by the
Spirit of the Lord. (2 Corinthians 3:17-18, NKJV)

12

Learning How to Love

Lois: We are not always right. That is such a shock. Our perceptions are not always true.

What about "the look"? You walk into church and someone across the pews from you gives you "the look." What did she mean by that? Was that a "you're not looking so good" look or a "I'm looking better than you" look? Then there are times when we do the "Oh, yes, I'm so glad to be here with you and this is so wonderful" look. But the look is phony because it doesn't match our true feelings.

Do you remember being taught "If you can't say something nice, don't say anything at all"? In our mature Christian niceness, we don't say that unkind word—we just let our feelings be known with a look. Many hearts have been broken over a careless look. It is so true that what is inside us can be seen more clearly on the outside than we would ever imagine. We can get ourselves in lots of trouble (sin!) by putting others down through a glance.

In the same vein, we can get ourselves in trouble when we misinterpret the looks of others!

Be very careful with perceptions. So many times I think I know everything about a situation . . . and I don't.

I have a dear best friend, Sharon Buckner. We met in high school, roomed together in college and now we both live in Colstrip. A friendship of over forty years is a wonderful treasure. I was acting as the master of ceremonies for a retirement event at the country club. Sharon walked in the door and gave me a look. I just knew that look meant, "Oh, there's Lois up front again." It seemed to me to definitely have been a negative look. (I had been "up front" a lot lately at social functions.) Two days later I met Sharon on the street. We were driving in opposite directions. I kind of slowed down to wave and pull to a stop. She whipped right on by me. Now I knew there was something wrong. Somehow I must have done something to offend her.

Once a year we spend a weekend together in the Bighorn Mountains of Wyoming. I tried to test out her voice while we were talking about planning the trip to see if she was going to back out or not. She seemed OK about going.

Yet on the drive down, she said that sometimes she wondered if we should keep doing this or not. I thought, *I knew she would say that.* I told her I thought we ought to talk about it when we got settled in up at the mountain. We built a fire and sat by it discussing a myriad of topics. Finally, with my heart thumping in my chest, I said, "I think we best talk about our friendship. I sense there is something wrong between us. Even your asking if I want to continue with this annual retreat is a signal to me that something is amiss. Could you tell me what is wrong?"

She looked at me in total shock. As I went over the supposed allegations, she grabbed my hand. "There is *nothing* wrong, Lois." She went on to tell me that she had been tired the night of the retirement dinner at the country club. She didn't want to go . . . and then even had to drive. Then she and her husband had had one of those little parking lot (been there, done that!) tiffs. They had a few words. They walked into the dinner, neither one pleased with the turn of events. She thought that by looking at me I would know the kind of day she had! That was the look I misinterpreted.

She went on to say she never knows vehicles. (And I knew that!) We have had our truck for three years. She didn't even know it was blue! She was not ignoring me by meeting me on the street and not stopping; she didn't even know it was me! (You can tell we live in a small town by the fact that we felt we could stop to visit on the street!) "Those smoky tinted windows don't help, either," she said, laughing.

* * *

An overactive imagination can get us in trouble too. Sometimes we have low self-esteem in certain areas that make us vulnerable to untruth. Sharon and I were having a soul-searching conversation just the other day over a cup of coffee. She had just received an offer to display some of her photography publicly. "The big surprise to me," she said, "is that I am not jumping with joy."

"Well, you should be," I admonished quickly. "Your work is good. You judge your work too harshly."

After a sip or two of coffee she added, "You know what I think it really is? I think I am afraid people won't like it. They will wonder how that photograph ever made it into the show." She looked at me. "How do you handle it? Surely not everyone who reads your column likes it. How do you personally deal with that?"

I explained that we all do things that others may not like. But you concentrate on doing your best and forge ahead. "If we all waited until we were perfect . . . at writing, painting, acting, singing, whatever—we'd never ever do anything creative in public," I said.

Together we decided that being accepted and having our talents appreciated is a desire we all have. When we are first putting our work "on the line" for the public, we all may feel insecure. At first, anyway. That's why authors race to read reviews of their books and actors anxiously await the reports of the critics. We finished our coffee.

I encouraged her as we walked to the car. "I think you should just be thrilled to be chosen for this honor. Don't compare yourself with others. Just enjoy the fact you have this chance. I think your work is great and so do lots of other people I know."

On my way home I thought about how insecure I feel at times. Knowing that the Bible says God loves me has helped me tremendously. I am so glad that we do not have to be perfect to earn His love.

We don't have to be the best Sunday school teacher or the best church pianist in order for Him to love us and use us. Romans 5:8 says, "While we were still sinners, Christ died for us." We can launch out. With our talents. With our relationships. Letting ourselves be vulnerable to the opinion of others. Knowing that we won't always please everyone.

I drove into my driveway and turned off the car. I sat with my hand on the wheel several minutes. I was wondering who didn't like my column.

* * *

I constantly have to remind myself that I do not know everything about everything! Things are not always what they seem and things change! In Montana, snowstorms come on silent wings quietly covering the meadows and mountains, or they come with a blast, blowing blustery gales of snow on our landscape. People who visit our state ask of sunshine or snow, "Is this typical weather?"

We natives answer, "We haven't seen 'typical' weather for a number of years." I believe that is true in many places in our world. Dry climates have flooding; wetlands are experiencing drought. Scientists have lots of theories and we will leave that to them. We are getting more accustomed to the fact that some things that were always the same—change.

One of the last really big snowstorms at our place was in April of 1997. It came at the same time our first granddaughter was being born in a hospital eighty miles away. Taryn is the first girl in my husband's family in sixty-five years and the first girl on my side in thirty-three years, so you can imagine our excitement. We couldn't see her right away. We had Justin and Tyler, the other grandkids, with us . . . snowed in. The snow came up to the hood of our pickup. We weren't going anywhere. Drifts were six to ten feet deep. Justin said, "Is it clear up to Grampi's chest or his waist?"

I looked out where Robert was shoveling a path, "The drift is up to Grampi's chest. I can see him out by the root cellar."

He thought about it a bit. "Well, there isn't much difference between his waist and his chest, right, Grammi?"

I laughed. "You're right. It's very deep either way!"

I thought about the slight difference later and laughed again. It is all relative, I guess, depending on what you are measuring. It reminded me of a revelation that came to me recently. I was thinking about churches, how we categorize them by denomination. Here a Catholic, there a Catholic. Here a Baptist, there a Baptist. Here a Pentecostal, there a Lutheran, here a Methodist, there a Presbyterian church.

If you are in that spot as you read this—visit several churches in your area and pray as you look. Check to see if the church follows biblical standards. Are the people friendly and interested in following and growing with Jesus? Ask for a statement of faith from the leaders. Check it out with your Bible. Ask Christian people whom you respect for their opinion. Speak to some of the people who attend there. Visit a few of their services. Lastly, check out their needs. Visit with the leadership. Could you, and your family, if you have one, offer help in certain areas of ministry? Do they have needs that are "right up your alley"? Pray. Pray. Pray. Ask God and then be faithful to serve with enthusiasm and joy where He directs you. What a blessing you will be to that church!

Don't be guilty of "judging a book (church) by its cover (name)!" My revelation was this: Be cautious about putting churches in denominational boxes. Not all Methodist churches are the same, as not all Baptist churches are the same. Not all Christian and Missionary Alliance churches are the same. Churches vary by the folks who attend there and the administrative staff. Even the part of the country they are located in makes differences.

So often we are guilty of judging a body of believers simply by their denominational title. How unfair. That is similar to judging them by the style of building in which they worship. God talked about the lives of the believers and the reputation of a few churches with John in the book of Revelation. That will clue any reader into the standards God has for our churches. You will notice He does not give them denominational names. He lists them by communities.

Oh, that we could learn to work together in "one accord" in our individual churches, and that the "one accord" could spread throughout our community! The common bond of Christ. Churches working together in unity can bring glory to God in our cities and towns.

Oh Lord, grant that we would spend more time in prayer for the "other" churches in our communities. Forgive us for the judgments and critical attitudes that often have more importance in our minds than your divine purpose of glorifying You! Might our love for one another shine brightly from church to church and denomination to denomination in our world. In Jesus' name, Amen.

* * *

Sometimes we can be talking about something happening in another church—and not even know what we are talking about!

For example, at our church Bible study on Wednesday night, a game show was played, the pastor broke down and cried, and suckers were all around the study table.

Sounds wild, doesn't it? Even blasphemous? Let me tell you what really happened. We were studying the 5th chapter of Judges. Pastor Gerry asked us if we could remember the cycle of five S's that repeat themselves over and over in the book of Judges. We guessed the first one: Sin.

Then I guessed, "Slipping and sliding?" Wrong. It was slavery. Sin brings slavery to one's life. We were all stumped for the third.

"What happens when you are burdened in your sin?" asked Pastor Gerry. "How do you reach for help?"

"Supplication," someone said. Then we had to think of the fourth. Who do we call on when we need forgiveness for our sin? We got that one. Our Savior.

Alas, the fifth S really had us guessing. "Give us some more hints," we said.

"When the Israelites were following God as they should, peace reigned in their land and there was . . .?"

"Silence!" Silence is the fifth S in the cycle repeated over and over in Judges. Oh how we all long for silence from the commotion of life around us. We yearn for peace in our lives.

"This is just like a television game show," someone else said. "Do we get a prize?"

"Yes, there are prizes," said Terri, "I have suckers for everyone!" With that she pulled out the most delicious sour apple caramel lollipops for us.

Yum! Seeing he was fast losing his students to the delights of their treats (just like little kids), Pastor said, "All right, let's get start . . ." and promptly choked on his words around the sucker in his mouth.

He coughed and choked. Until the tears were streaming down his face. He got his handkerchief. Finally he could speak again, amid thankful nervous laughter. So you see? At our Bible study, we had a game show. There were suckers around the table. The pastor broke down and cried. A silly illustration? Yes, but it proves that sometimes innocent situations can be misinterpreted with disastrous results.

It immediately brought a lesson to my mind. How often in real life do we hear only part of a story and jump to erroneous conclusions? This little incident was all in fun. However, sometimes a similar occurrence can hurt someone. A few facts cleverly or unconsciously told without the whole story can damage a reputation. Sometimes just seeing a person in a certain place can cause us to jump to a conclusion that is in reality not true.

I was reminded how easy it is to make wrong judgments about someone else. Much easier than believing the best, and expecting the best in our fellow humans. Which brings me right back to the lesson from Judges. When we sin, we can slip and slide right into slavery; or we can make supplication to our Savior, receiving salvation and peace in the form of silence from grief in our souls. Good, huh?

* * *

"Put it wight dere."

"OK."

"My turn now," grins the toddler. He has a red block in his hand. He carefully sets it on the stack of multicolored blocks between them.

"Your turn." His little friend picks a blue block next. They continue taking turns. Their tower gets taller. Across the room two others are lying on their tummies with a coloring book.

BANG! CRASH!

Everyone in the nursery looks toward the tower. Or rather where the tower was. The eyes of the two builders are teary. Billy is standing in the pile of blocks. He has his tough look on his little pudgy face. Kicking down the tower wasn't enough. He runs over to the kids on the floor and grabs the coloring book off the floor. "Mine!" he shouts over his shoulder as he runs away.

We were required to spend nine hours a week observing the children in the college nursery as a lab for our child development class. We analyzed behaviors and wrote reports. I have forgotten the reports, the questions and the exams. I have never forgotten the hours of observation. There were the Givers and the Takers. There were the Builders and the Wreckers. Davy would share anything including his bottle. His favorite line was " 'Et's pay, OK?" He was always bending down in the face of someone asking if they wanted to play.

Thirty years later I have observed some of the same behavior patterns in adults that were charted back then on my reports. I see people who seem to relish destructive gossip (all in the guise of concern, of course). Others "get a kick" out of making someone the brunt of a cruel joke. Not-so-subtle innuendoes are used to break up families or cause division at work or school or in a church. Some people seem to thrive on tearing things apart and causing others grief.

I have appreciated the opposites of that behavior, the peacemakers, like Davy, those who have the gifts of hospitality and forgiveness and compassion. Those who are always there to say a good word about someone being maligned. Those who love and keep on loving. Those who are there to lift up the fallen and rebuild the block towers.

Are you a Davy?

We all have our bad times. We have our sandpaper days when things are going rough. I have torn down more than one colorful block tower in my adult life. I am not proud of it either. I had to ask forgiveness and make amends.

A friend once said to me, "You have two choices in your daily walk. You can tear things down, or you can build bridges. It is up to you." That same choice is ours on our path of joy.

I'd like to share some blocks with you today. Shall we build a bridge? You stack the yellow ones. I'll do red. " 'Et's pay, OK?"

* * *

Robert and I went over to a Labor Day retreat being held at Camp Bethel, which is just across the road from our place in the Bighorn Mountains. Pastor Dave Mathieson, First Baptist Church, Broadus, Montana was speaking that day. He talked about how sometimes things spread in the church and the pastor is often the last to know. He said that sometimes gossip could run through a congregation like a runaway loop of wire snaking from pew to pew.

He wondered who would be the one to cut the loop. I prayed then and there, "Lord, let me be the one to cut the loop. Let me not enjoy passing along an untruth! Forgive me for the times I have willingly been a part of the loop! Amen."

* * *

Sometimes we need to prefer one another over ourselves. Sometimes we must have "passionate patience" to go into a friendship a little longer.

What would happen if you become that person's friend? Only God knows. Are you willing to give it a chance?

My Friend Karen

From my faithful old notebook,
I turned back the pages and took a long look.

'Twas an answer to prayer, our friendship, you see,
Because I prayed to God for a friend who's a Christian
      like me.
From right here in town, God showed Karen Woods,
      a sister-in-Christ, to me.
I said, "Oh God, she's too perfect to be a real friend.
      Perfect I can't be!"

But she had a Ross,
   And I did too.
She had three perfect sons,
   And I did too.
She had a husband who's a 10,
   And I did too.
She had a personal relationship with God,
   And I did too.
She was interested in growing with God,
   And I was too.
And that little cocoon of friendship began to blossom
      on a tree . . .

     and I learned . . .
She was into health foods,
   And I wasn't.
She was into makeup,
   And I wasn't.
She kept grocery lists and menus,
   And I didn't.
She was a whiz at the family budget,

And I wasn't.
She could sing like a canary,
   And I couldn't.
She was a Cleanie,
   And I wasn't . . .
       and that was OK!

      and she told me . . .
I was creative,
   And she wasn't.
I was artistic,
   And she wasn't.
I was a garage sale expert,
   And she wasn't.
I had a microwave oven,
   And she didn't.
I was a group organizer,
   And she wasn't . . .
       and that was OK!

And then the butterflies spread their wings into friendship.

I started clipping coupons and making menus,
   And she had a garage sale.
I started to sing in the choir,
   And she was the leader of the group.
I made grocery lists and started a budget,
   And her creativity blossomed and grew.

I purchased vitamins and makeup,
   And she purchased a microwave oven.
I started to exercise and drink herbal tea,
   And she became a teacher with a classroom of kids . . .
       and that was OK!

118

Learning How to Love

and we learned . . .

Her house sometimes got messy,
    And my house sometimes got cleaned.
Her boys weren't really always perfect,
    And my boys weren't really always perfect.
She organized her day by schedule,
    And I organized my day by schedule.
She loved God and Bible studies and prayer,
    And I loved God and Bible studies and prayer.

And sometimes we would toss out the schedules and lists and
        we would drink herbal tea,
And talk about God and Bible studies and ideas and blessings
        and husbands and kids,
And the past, and the present, and the future, and pray . . .

And that was OK!

Lois Olmstead © 1988

119

13

Our Witness to the World

Lois: Phyllis and I accentuate the similarities between us. That's how friendship works. We both love being grandmas. We still love drinking coffee together. We talk and visit. We love sharing what God is teaching each of us individually. We love shopping together. And . . . we love eating out.

We still have differences. We tread softly and love lots. We don't agree on everything . . . and that's OK. I still can't sing and she still can't paint. People still call her for prayer. They still call me to teach.

We both still do dumb things . . .

She had all these dishes in her sink one day. She put the plug in the sink, put the soap in and turned on the water. When the water came on she remembered that she needed to move the sprinkler hose in the garden. She noticed on the way back that the flower bed needed to be weeded. So, thinking she should do things as they appear and need to be done, she weeded the flower bed. As she finished, she realized the plants needed water. She thought maybe she should water them too . . .

"EEK! WATER!"

She suddenly remembered the water in the kitchen. She went running, well, sliding back into the kitchen. The water had run down the counter and through all the drawers, under the toaster, behind the coffeepot, down the wall, soaking the rugs and everything.

By the time she got done with the cleanup she had the cleanest kitchen in Colstrip! She ran downstairs to put the towels and rugs in the washing machine. Then she decided to do the dishes . . . and not move this time. She put the plug in the sink, put the soap in and turned on the water. While the water was running, the phone rang. It was her sister Linda from Ohio. She couldn't hear for the water running . . . so she stepped around the corner into the bathroom. . . .

God gives us some lessons twice!

Phyllis: Do you remember the little house up the "holler" in West Virginia? It was fun living up the river. It was more than just swimming at the "Willow Hole" all summer. By watching the river out the kitchen window, you could see the seasons come and go.

In the winter, the ice would crack, pop and break up. Sometimes as the ice backed up, the river would overflow its banks. The river, out of control, was always scary. Then spring came with lots of rain (we'd grab our quilt and head for the porch swing), and everything turned green and flowers began to bloom. I loved the springtime. The birds came and sang promises of summer to come.

Summer would arrive in all of its splendor. The rocks in the river would begin to show their heads above the water. The river that flooded during the winter and spring would get so dry that you could walk across on those rocks.

Autumn would come to give the river a drink of water once again. The red, gold and brown leaves would fall from the trees and sail like colorful boats downstream to their destination. Then back to winter.

As the river worked its way through town, every eye watched it at one time or another. Some mocked it as "such a little river." Others who had seen its fury during the flood times held respect for the river as it passed their porches.

The river was across the road from Mom's house. Up behind the house where no one could see was her spring. It was a small spring that provided for our everyday needs. It was only about two feet across and flowed from beneath a big rock. It gave us water to cook with and a cool drink in the hot summer months.

The spring gave water for cleansing, whether it was our dirty faces or our feed sack dresses. Mom just laid the pipe in the spring and ran it to the house. She protected the spring and always had a piece of screen over the end of the pipe to keep the dirt and twigs out.

When we went out to play, Mom always reminded us, "Don't you girls go near the spring, and be sure you keep the dog out of it!" She realized the importance of it in our lives.

Sometimes Mom would turn on the water at the sink, and instead of the clear, sparkling water, out would run a stream of brown. Sometimes no water came out at all. Mom would run to the spring, get down on her knees and take away from the pipe all the leaves and sticks that were blocking the flow of water.

That little tiny spring never went dry in the fifty years Mom lived there. The river would run almost dry during the hot summer months, but the little spring always supplied our need.

The overflow that didn't come through the pipe went on past the yard, down around the garden and into the south fork of the Cherry River. Down at the old swinging bridge the north fork and south fork merged to form the Cherry River. A few miles down the road the Cherry met with the Cranberry and joined the Gauley River. Somewhere on down through the mountains and hills the Gauley merged with the New River and formed the Big Kanawha River, which eventually went into the Ohio and on and on. Mom's little spring was a part of all this.

That's how it is with us and the Lord. If we have asked Jesus Christ to be our Savior, we have the spring of Living Water within us. It flows from the Rock. It is a faithful spring that never runs dry.

He is always there to meet our every need.
He will cleanse us when we are stained.
He will quench our thirst when we are thirsty.
He is the life-giving water for our souls.
Fresh, clean, clear, unending supply of Living Water.

As the Holy Spirit flows through us, we need to protect that gift and cherish it. We need to keep the pipe unplugged. It can become plugged with control, criticism, jealousy and resentment. Hurt, bitterness, anger, pride, independence, self-righteousness and fear can also block the flow, as can so much other debris of life.

We need to run to the spring, get down on our knees and let Him take away the things that are plugging the pipe. This will allow the Living Water, the Holy Spirit, to flow through us individually. The overflow can then flow out of us, into the family, into the church, into the town, the community and throughout the county and the state.

It's the River—the river of the Holy Spirit.

Mama's spring flowed with cleansing for our bodies, our clothes and our home. Jesus, the Living Water has started, and will finish, the cleansing in me.

Through the years, He has revealed sin in my life as I walked day by day. He has forgiven me and cleansed me as I repented. He has healed old hurts that still affected my thinking and attitude in certain situations. He has released me from bondage when the struggles were more than I could handle on my own, as He works as the "author and finisher of our faith" (Hebrews 12:2, NKJV).

One Sunday morning in church we stood and began to sing a song about the Lord's tenderness, about receiving His love. And I felt a melting of my heart as Love poured in, and bitterness slithered out the door.

As Fred and I settled our differences God's way, Unforgiveness packed his bag and left, no longer a welcome guest. Deep-seated hurts of rejection and physical and verbal abuse were healed as His love and acceptance flowed. Fear no longer had a hiding place as the Light of the World shone into the darkest corner of my heart. Loneliness was replaced by Jesus, who says, "Never will I leave you; never will I forsake you" (Hebrews 13:5).

The Lord has continued through the years to erase the things from the blackboard of my life that were contrary to His plan for me. The Spirit of Truth is revealing that which Lies and Deception had concealed.

At last, one day, God exposed and removed in the powerful name of Jesus the root of hatred and anger buried deep in my heart. In First Corinthians 4:5, His Word says the Lord will "bring to light the hidden things of darkness and reveal the counsels of the hearts" (NKJV). Sometimes it's amazing what He finds when we ask Him to "search my heart."

The Lord Jesus Christ
   —my Savior
      —my Healer
         —my Deliverer
            —my Lord.

The cleansing continues day by day as He molds me and shapes me more into His image. Am I completely cleansed today? I doubt it.

Am I totally free? I don't know. All I know at this point is—I am cleaner and freer today than I have ever been in my life! As the Living Water flows, the words of the old hymn ring so true:

Peace like a river—
  Flows through my soul—
    I've been forgiven—
      Cleansed and made whole.

Thank You, Jesus!

Do you see how important it is that we are faithful and obedient to keep our hearts clean? His faithfulness is still there. He says He will never leave us nor forsake us. It's our responsibility to clean the pipes and keep the flow moving. There is a world that we need to reach.

Just as part of Mom's little spring is part of the big rivers that eventually reach the coast, so are we, as individuals, part of the River of Life. Remember His faithfulness. The Living Water never runs dry, and He supplies our every need.

 ois:

Shout for joy to the LORD, all the earth.
Worship the LORD with gladness;
  come before him with joyful songs.
Know that the LORD is God.
  It is he who made us, and we are his;
  we are his people, the sheep of his pasture.

Enter his gates with thanksgiving
  and his courts with praise;
  give thanks to him and praise his name.

For the LORD is good and his love endures forever;
  his faithfulness continues through all generations.
    (Psalm 100)

How do we keep our joy? How do we keep our pipes from being plugged? Pastor Schaefer used to say, "Keep your eyes on Jesus." It seems like such a simplistic thing, but it keeps us on the right path. We can have contented, contagious joy when our minds and eyes are on Jesus. It is important we keep our eyes on Jesus—not on each other.

We are each a beautiful part of God's plan. Someone told me once that we should keep the main thing the main thing. Whatever matters much to God should matter much to us. He wants us to take the gospel to others.

> Ye are the salt of the earth: but if the salt have lost his savour, wherewith shall it be salted? it is thenceforth good for nothing, but to be cast out, and to be trodden under foot of men. Ye are the light of the world. A city that is set on an hill cannot be hid. Neither do men light a candle, and put it under a bushel, but on a candlestick; and it giveth light unto all that are in the house. Let your light so shine before men, that they may see your good works, and glorify your Father which is in heaven. (Matthew 5:13-16, KJV)

We are to tell people outside the family of God that Jesus died for us, that our sins can be forgiven, that we can have eternal life, that He's coming to take us home with Him. Those are the things that are the main thing with Him and should be the main thing with us.

- If we are consumed by the turmoil of broken relationships, how can we go out and tell the world about the gospel?

- If we can't forgive each other, how can we talk to others about God's forgiveness?

One of the main things that Jesus rebuked while He was here on earth was being a hypocrite. Are we being hypocrites in our own churches? Woe to us! We have to keep the main thing the main thing. We need to keep our eyes focused on Jesus. When we have our eyes focused on Jesus, we won't have time to worry about what everybody else is doing. That keeps our attitudes right and our actions right.

Robert and I had the opportunity to hear Dr. John Piper of Desiring God Ministries at a national convention in Charlotte, North Carolina in 1998. He is the pastor in an inner-city church in Minneapolis, Minnesota. His challenge revealed a weakness in my walk with the Lord. His words inspired me to spend more time listening to my Heavenly Father. Please read what touched my soul:

Let me begin where we left off last night by trying to clarify one of those key sentences, namely God is most glorified in us when we are most satisfied in Him.

As I read the Bible there are two great passions that are expressed. One is God's passion for His glory, which we focused on heavily last night, and the other is the passion of the human heart to be happy.

That psalm that was just quoted in the prayer said, "Satisfy us in the morning with Your steadfast love that we may rejoice and be glad in You all of our days."

I believe that prayer, "Satisfy me, O God, in the morning that I may rejoice and be glad in You all my days" is the deepest cry of the human heart.

Now most people don't know how to pray it. They say, "Satisfy me." They say it to money. They say it to prestige. They say it to style. They say it to marriage partners. They say it to children. They say it to their jobs—Satisfy me. Satisfy me.

And the only prayer that works is to address it to God and say, "Satisfy me in the morning with thy steadfast love, that I may rejoice and be glad in Thee all the days of my life."

So there are these two great passions in the universe: the passion of the human heart to be happy and the passion of God to be glorified. And I have spent most of my adult life since my seminary days trying to understand how those two things relate to each other. And everything I have ever written and every talk I have ever given has more or less been an effort to bring them together.

Because I see the Bible bringing them together . . . and that sentence that I quoted last night and just a moment ago, is my best effort to date of bringing them together.

God is most glorified in you when you are most satisfied in Him. Which means the gospel that we have to bring to the world is that these two great passions are not at odds, but in a most marvelous and glorious way come to simultaneous fruition in the act of delighting in God.

God is glorified when you are satisfied in Him.

The way you glorify a spring of living water is not by hauling buckets of your own self-wrought labor up from the valleys of humanity and dumping them there in the spring and saying, "There. Be enriched, O Spring."

The way you glorify a spring is by recognizing how thirsty you are . . . and forsaking every other kind of drink, walking to the spring, falling prostrate before the spring and drinking in the water and saying, "Ah-h-h-h." And in the strength of the spring beckoning others to join you in it. (Dr. John Piper, Pastor, Bethlehem Baptist Church. Used by permission.)

I saw myself in Dr. Piper's words. I was so busy filling the spring with buckets of my "own self-wrought labor" that I wasn't really spending time at the spring. Isn't that just like us?

We need to spend time with God, listening, focusing on Him, getting our spirit under the control of His Spirit, our will in tune with His will. Then our lives change, our joy is full, our motives are pure and our reactions become God-honoring. We are under His power and not our own.

God has a family of beautiful people, each individually created and molded uniquely by the Master Potter. Sometimes I think the greatest tragedy in America today is people trying to be like each other. God created each of us individually. He has a plan for us that can outdistance any plans we have.

* * *

I planted a garden this year. In southeastern Montana where we live, there is little water. So I made a little garden on a hill circled by rocks that I could water with my dishwater. I did not plant just one kind of flower—I planted many different kinds. Some, like the yucca, are native to our country.

There is a bitterroot from Big Piney, Wyoming. I brought it home in a paper cup and it bloomed all summer long. I planted chives, petunias and peonies. I have taken five rolls of film of the flower garden. I have sent pictures to everyone.

It is beautiful because the plants are all different. Some have blossoms, some do not. Some are tall and some are short. They are all unique and look awesome together.

God has a flower garden too. He has us. It takes each one of us individually to add beauty to His garden. We can go out into the world to share His love. The "petunias" go one place, the "roses" go another because there are all different kinds of people out there.

People from church homes
  and broken homes,

from up the creek
    and down the holler.

They are waiting everywhere for others to come share God's love.

*Go therefore and make disciples of all the nations, baptizing
them in the name of the Father and of the Son and of the Holy
Spirit, teaching them to observe all things that I have
commanded you; and lo, I am with you always, even to
the end of the age. (Matthew 28:19-20, NKJV)*

Denim and Lace

You created us, Lord
You called us by name
Each one is different
No two are the same
Molded in Your image
Walking in Your grace
We're Sunflowers or Roses
We are Denim—and we are Lace.

Phyllis Rowe © 2000

14

With Thankful Hearts

Lois and Phyllis: God made a difference in our lives; in saving us and restoring our friendship. God can make a difference in your life too. None of this would have happened if we'd had our own way and went our own way.

One of the things we got out of this broken relationship and restoration was spiritual growth. Most of life's lessons don't come from the classroom; they come from the trenches, from everyday life and everyday things. Life is so short; we have to get back to reaching the hurting.

We learned so much from this experience about depending on God, being willing to change and willing to ask for forgiveness. In our case, the cancer caused us to get serious about our broken relationship. And we thank God that we did.

In *Filled with the Spirit . . . Then What?*, Mabel Francis wrote,

> While He was nailed to the cross, the crowd shouted to Him to come down. If He would do this, they said, they would believe that He was the Messiah. But He was drinking a bitter cup and He knew that He had to stay there until He was dead—six long hours!

If we could die immediately in regard to self, it would be much easier!

However, we need time to see all the traits of self and to consign them to the cross one by one—until we have died to all of them. That is what makes it hard.

But how blessed to know now, that instead of going into a spiritual slump when I saw these threats of self, I was to thank God for showing them to me and bring them directly to Him and trust Him to give deliverance at every point. (Christian Publications, pp. 16-17)

So, we thank God for showing them to us and bringing us into a right relationship with each other, but more importantly with Him.

Christians need a wake-up call on how important reaching the lost really is. Life is short and people are lost. We need to be carrying the message of God's love and forgiveness to them.

Pure water is unpolluted, free and clean. We want to be vessels God uses to take His Word to someone else. You don't want to be a plugged-up pipe. You want to be ready to be available, to be used by God. Every morning this should be our focus. As Pastor Schaefer said, "Keep your eyes on Jesus." We have to get back to what is really essential. We are called to be His servants, spreading His truth and love.

We are all different. Just like a flower garden, there is beauty in the differences. Be careful not to pull a flower out, thinking it's a weed! God made each one of us unique. He tells us so in His Word, the Bible.

We believe the Bible is the inspired Word of God. It tells the stories of the lives of real women and real men—people just like us. Naomi was a real person. Elizabeth was a real person. So were Ruth and Esther and Dorcas and Eve. These were real living women. And Joseph, David, Jehoshaphat and Peter were real people too. The Bible tells us their stories.

And now we have told you our story.

May God receive all the glory, honor and praise.

To contact **Lois** about a speaking engagement,
write to her at:

P.O. Box 907
Colstrip, Montana 59323

or e-mail her at

olmstead@mcn.net

To contact **Phyllis** about a speaking engagement,
write to her at:

P.O. Box 896
Colstrip, Montana 59323

or e-mail her at

wrowe@mcn.net

Lois Olmstead shares her faith in God and her optimistic and amusing views on life with women's groups across America. She is the author of two other books, *Breast Cancer and Me* and *Enjoying the Journey*. Lois and her husband, Robert, live in Colstrip, Montana.

Phyllis Rowe was born into a family of five girls in the "hills and hollers" of West Virginia. In addition to speaking at seminars, she is a gifted soloist. Phyllis and her husband, Jim, also live in Colstrip, Montana